AUTISM WITH A
SIDE OF SUSHI

AUTISM WITH A SIDE OF SUSHI

A STORY OF A JAPANESE MOM AND HER SON ON THE SPECTRUM

KURI YASUNO

NEW DEGREE PRESS
COPYRIGHT © 2021 KURI YASUNO
All rights reserved.

INTERIOR ARTWORK CREATED BY *Kuri Yasuno*

AUTISM WITH A SIDE OF SUSHI
A story of a Japanese mom and her son on the spectrum

ISBN   979-8-88504-915-3   *Paperback*
        979-8-88504-741-8   *Kindle Ebook*
        979-8-88504-220-8   *Ebook*

For my boys,
Seth, Daniel, Greg
&
Lucky

CONTENTS

INTRODUCTION		9
CHAPTER 1.	AUTISM, SUSHI, AND OUR STORY	13
CHAPTER 2.	SURROUNDED BY NOISE	23
CHAPTER 3.	CAN'T FIND IT? CREATE IT.	35
CHAPTER 4.	SWIM! SWIM! SWIM!	49
CHAPTER 5.	TO TELL OR NOT TO TELL	63
CHAPTER 6.	OPERATION GRANOLA BAR	81
CHAPTER 7.	QUIRKS FOR GOOD NOT EVIL	95
CHAPTER 8.	FIND A HOBBY, GET A DOG	109
CHAPTER 9.	EVEN DAYS AND ODD DAYS	121
CHAPTER 10.	FAMILY VACATIONS	129
	CONCLUSION	143
	ACKNOWLEDGMENTS	151
	APPENDIX	155

INTRODUCTION

When I asked my son, Daniel, if I could write a book about autism to tell stories about us, he hesitated. He asked me why I wanted to write it. I explained I have always wanted to write a book, and I thought I wanted to discuss autism. I hoped by sharing our experiences with autism, we could teach people about the autism spectrum. The more people learn about it, the more accepting they may become.

I gave him the day to think about it. At dinner, Daniel said, "Sure, you can write this book. If it's going to help people be nicer, then yes, I want you to write it."

I started outlining topics and laying out Post-its with my notes. I made lists of the positives, the negatives, the things I had learned, the things I had struggled with, and everything in between. Finally, I put pen to paper and unloaded the thoughts and stories that were swirling in my brain. I received approval to write the book from my publisher, was assigned an editor, and submitted my chapters one by one.

As I was close to completing and sending off the middle section of the manuscript, Daniel and I got into a big fight. An argument over him yelling at me in the mornings morphed into me saying something obnoxious about having more content to add to the negative behaviors chapter. Furious, Daniel had the last word with, "Well, fine then, you can't write your book."

I was stunned. My book was cancelled. I was crushed. By this time, I had poured hours and hours into this project, I was hearing great things from my editor, and I was feeling like I could produce an actual book. I was so close to getting it done.

Daniel was mad when I mentioned the chapter on negative behaviors because he realized I had the audacity to write about his, well, negative behaviors. How could I possibly include anything about his tantrums? He declared that the stories about his outbursts would be embarrassing, thus I could not write about them. I was furious, aggravated, and then deflated. I couldn't fault him for not wanting to be embarrassed. I was writing the story of our lives—not just mine, but his, too—so I had to respect his wishes. The book, the dream, was over. I asked him, "What if I changed our names? No one would know it's us." Daniel stood steadfast and said he didn't want "those stories out there."

After a cooling-off period of about a week, I asked him what he was mad about, specifically. Daniel said he didn't like the stories about his extreme rigidity being made public. I considered this. One of the points of the book was to share the ups and downs of our journey, and a major part of that—the latter half of elementary school and all of middle school—had to do with his rigidity. If I couldn't include that, what was the point? So, I let it go. I sulked for an entire day and made sure Daniel saw my disappointment. The next day, I told my editor the book would not see the light of day.

After a few more days, and because I am forever the optimist, I decided to try one more thing. By this time, we had made up and were back to our regular selves. I asked Daniel to sit with me as I went chapter by chapter and asked him if I could write about the things in them. I told him my goal was not to embarrass him, and that whatever content he did not like, I would delete it. Daniel agreed.

We went through and scanned the pages, deleting some stories and keeping others. I was surprised at what was cut and what was not, but I kept my opinions to myself. At one point, Daniel started to get bored and asked, "Mom, how much longer is this book? Why did you write so much?"

Then we got to a section about Daniel constantly putting his hand on his younger brother's head. This one habit of Daniel's was the source of years of bickering, fighting, and angst. When I mentioned that he used to do that, he laughed and said, "Oh, yeah! Remember that? Ahahahahaha!" Four or five years of my life were summarized by him laughing at the source of my pain. As soul crushing as it was, it was also kind of funny. We got through the chapters and I was given a new go-ahead. I rewrote the second half of the manuscript. I am still disappointed that some of the chapters had to go, especially the potty-training one.

This book started with excitement. I had so many ideas and I felt like the possibilities were endless. The stages went from the joy of creating something and almost seeing it through to the crushing blow of defeat as it was cancelled followed by filling the glass half full to consider some options and then ending with the final resolution after compromise. I realized this writing experience captured the exact spirit of the relationship I have with my son and his autism.

Everyone's autism is different, thus everyone's story is, too. It is important for me to be clear that I am not speaking for all people who have been affected by autism. This is our autism journey, the one I share with Daniel.

CHAPTER 1

AUTISM, SUSHI, AND OUR STORY

"Ewwwww! You eat that? Isn't that, like, raw fish and seaweed? That's disgusting."

I heard this exclamation a lot growing up. The Americans I met in the 1980s thought the idea of raw fish wrapped in rice and seaweed was far from appetizing.

I was five years old when my family moved to America for my father's career. During the same week, we moved into a two-story house, and I was enrolled into a public elementary school in Long Island, New York. Until that first day, I had never seen a person with eyes colored anything other than brown or hair other than black. I did not know a single English word except the phrase my mother armed me with in case there was trouble: "Shut your mouth, baby." In retrospect, I'm glad I did not have to try out that verbal attack.

So many things were different. I had never lived in a house before, let alone a house with stairs—two sets of stairs. One set went up to the second floor with its many bedrooms, and another went down to the basement. We had multiple entrances, so where should we put our shoes? In Japan, it is customary to take our shoes off when entering our homes. In our last home in Japan, we lived in apartments called mansions, but that did not translate literally, and it had only one entrance, where we would put our shoes. This house had three floors, three bathrooms, a garage, a yard, and even a working fireplace.

Everything was different. The language was different, the clothes were different, and even the mode of transportation was different. We had to drive places now. We had two cars. My mom had to learn how to drive.

At school, I was often asked about samurais with swords and women wearing kimonos. Usually, the conversation would move to food. The hot topic was always sushi and how it grossed out so many Americans.

Fast forward to today and look at us now. Fancy Japanese restaurants are thriving with extravagant sushi platters of raw fish, raw sea urchin, and eel. If you bring sushi to lunch, no one comments. Sushi started showing up in movies like *The Breakfast Club* with Molly Ringwald. Her sushi lunch was a status symbol. Going out to grab sushi is no longer gross but completely accepted as a social norm. Most food courts now have a sushi place right next to the Italian, the Chinese, or the burger place.

As the mother of a child who is autistic, my wish is for the world to think of autism more like sushi—something common yet unique. A staple in the Japanese diet, sushi is something we enjoy daily and as a celebratory treat. The truly special kind of sushi takes years of training and experience to create. It is respected and held in high regard. This is how I'd like to see autism evolve—not as something unknown and mysterious but as something everyone knows about and values.

If autism was like sushi, then when a parent mentioned a child on the spectrum, it would be treated as a unique and interesting trait. My hope is that, one day, the idea of autism will be so commonplace there will no longer be assumptions, generalizations, or fear surrounding it.

When our son, Daniel, was diagnosed, I was in shock. I had no idea how to absorb this information. What was this mysterious thing? Who gave it to him? Was it genetic? Was it my fault? Did I do something during pregnancy to have caused this? Was it deadly? Would my child grow up to be normal?

I had feelings of denial. He's not autistic. He's quirky. He gets stuck on certain topics, likes to quote movies, and has a hard time making friends, but that's not autism. That's just a young kid learning how to navigate life.

I also felt depressed. *Oh, woe is me. How can I handle this situation? I'm not equipped.* I was drowning in anxiety and frozen with fear. I spent a long time going down a deep, dark spiral. I was overwhelmed with fear of the future and the unknown, afraid I wouldn't be able to raise my son because I was unprepared.

Why did I have to have these feelings? I strongly believe the fear of autism comes from a lack of information, or access to information, about autism. And in this day of information saturation, I believe we can remedy this situation.

History has seen this phenomenon repeatedly. If you currently wear a seatbelt, you have been a part of it. In the 1980s, we saw a major push to get Americans to buckle their seat belts. When this campaign started, billboards and posters everywhere portrayed people buckling their seat belts. Pianists, a person getting a haircut, lifeguards, athletes, and all sorts of people were buckling up. It became normalized and common to buckle up. Today, it is rare to see someone not buckling up. This message has become so ingrained in society, and it has the added bonus of actually saving lives.

When a new parent gets a diagnosis that their child is on the spectrum, wouldn't it be great if the parent didn't start spiraling out of control with worry? What if being informed that a child is autistic was received the same way as the doctor saying, "Your child appears to be left-handed."

To get to this point, more people have to know more about autism. Normalizing autism starts with awareness. I like how Brené Brown says, "People are hard to hate up close." I see this as an invitation to meet, include, and become aware of people who are on the autism spectrum. Once you know someone who is on or raising a child on the autism spectrum, and once you start hearing the word, the whole concept becomes less foreign and more tangible. Once it's up close, you can't hate it. You start to accept it.

Sometimes, when you learn a new word, you start hearing it everywhere. If you learn about a new type of car, you start seeing it everywhere. Once you become aware of autism, you will see how it is a part of so many lives.

The big debate is whether to cure autism or create an environment where people who are autistic can thrive. Some people think curing autism implies it is something that needs fixing. This offends people who think autism does not need fixing. Some people argue about "a person with autism" versus "an autistic person." I say argue away. Talk about it. Bring up these discussions frequently with lots of different people. Make it so well-known that everyone will become familiarized with autism and no one can hate it, be cruel, or be mean to someone who is an autistic person or has autism.

I certainly know what it is like to stand out and be different. I grew up Japanese in America, the only Asian girl in my whole grade. I was raised by very traditional Japanese parents while speaking Japanese in our home with my brother. We ate Japanese food, read Japanese books, and watched the one Japanese channel that was available to us, NHK. I attended a regular American public school during the week and Japanese school on the weekends. My parents even subjected me to Japanese *juku,* which I liked to call After School School. I completed high school and University in the United States.

A few years after graduating from college, my older brother moved back to Japan as did my parents about a decade later. I stayed and met Greg. A few years later, Greg and I got married on a beach in Kauai. A few years after that, Daniel was born. Two years and twelve days later, Seth was born, and we became a family of four.

When Daniel was born, he was a crier. The second night at the hospital, I remember Greg telling me that all of the babies in the nursery were peacefully bundled and sleeping, except one. One baby was screaming his head off. That baby was Daniel—our Daniel. I used to say he was crying because he was airing his grievances. He was mad we took him out of the comforts of the womb, and he wanted us to put him back where it was warm and safe. He was just ticked off. I couldn't blame the little guy.

Having a first-time baby who cries a lot is zero fun. We quickly learned that incessant crying is called colic, and some babies are just born with it. Some doctors will say it's gas and give you gripe water drops. Others will tell you it's reflux and have you hold the baby vertically and suggest that you put them in a car seat to sleep. If you were nursing like I was, the meanest of the doctors will tell you to eliminate items from your diet like, *gasp,* chocolate because that could be irritating the baby through the breastmilk. As all moms of babies with cholic will tell you, you can hold them, rock them, or swaddle them, but they just cry. The only time they don't is when they are sleeping or being fed.

Luckily for us, Daniel was a very good sleeper. After crying for most of the day, he would fall asleep in a predictable pattern—a few hours of crying and then a few hours of sleeping. As soon as his eyes started to droop, we would turn on the soothing sounds of a roaring hair dryer. They say it imitates the sounds within the womb, where he was so desperately trying to get back to. Before Amazon was around, Greg found a CD with the sound of a hair dryer. This was a life saver. We cranked the CD and played it on repeat in his room. I remember freaking out every time the track would end and start over, giving us a terrifying moment of silence as we worried Daniel would wake up and start wailing until the CD started up again.

Greg and I have mostly been on the same page about raising Daniel. Neither of us thought twice at the idea of searching for a CD of hair dryer sounds. We also found CDs of vacuum cleaner sounds and other machines that made loud noises. I had no idea there was even a market for such odd items.

After we became experts at turning on the hair dryer CD and walking out quieter than a ninja, Daniel slowly started to come around. He got used to the idea of being out of the cozy womb and began to accept his fate here on Earth. We also got smart and learned some tricks. Daniel would not cry if I held him in my arms and bounced. As my arms would get very tired, I had to come up with an alternative. With our thinking caps on, Greg and I pulled out the big, green exercise ball. I bounced on this ball as I held Daniel in my arms. I spent a lot of time on that bouncy ball. We even traveled with it because that was the most certain way to get Daniel to fall asleep.

It became a fun game because the more vigorously I bounced, the more he enjoyed it. Daniel also loved singing. This was very fortuitous because I love to sing. I would sing everything and anything, but mostly show tunes. I sang a ton of "Suddenly Seymour" from *Little Shop of Horrors* and "There's a Place for Us" from *West Side Story*.

When Daniel was about four months old, the crying got less and less frequent, and he started becoming easier to figure out. He loved a routine. Wake up, change, nurse, play, nap, nurse, nap, activity, nurse, nap, bath, bed. As long as I was around, holding him or singing to him, he was pretty calm. He had a good amount of separation anxiety and pretty much hated anyone else, but other than that, he was a great sleeper and nurser.

At this stage, I couldn't do much with Daniel. Babies this young don't really play yet and they don't move around. So, I looked for some companionship in this new role as the person who watched a small human being all day, just trying to make it to the next day—other moms with lots of questions. To make new mom friends, I joined a local mothers group called PACE where I met ten other mothers. This was a weekly meeting where the moderators gave us timely parenting advice and then a social hour to talk, vent, and discuss baby issues like colic and nursing. This was the first place I saw babies the same age as Daniel and realized he was a bit different.

While the mentors and the moms took turns talking, Daniel was the only baby who couldn't be put down. He constantly had to be attached to me. As the other kids started to roll around and crawl, Daniel stayed stuck to me and didn't want to explore. On a physical developmental level, Daniel was the same as the other kids. He rolled over on time, he sat up on time, he crawled on time, he stood on time, and he also started walking at exactly one year old. This was the same across the board with these PACE friends.

The differences were more subtle. The other PACE babies started to point at objects they wanted to see or look at toys with their moms. The other kids would turn when they were called. The other kids were able to separate from their mothers. Daniel was the only one who struggled with these things.

I saw these differences but I didn't see them. I had a bit of a gut feeling that Daniel was different, but I hoped it was nothing. The PACE moms would organize walks together and I would watch as the other kids sat happily in their strollers flipping through soft cloth books or chewing on a toy. Daniel was not happy unless he was attached to me in the *BabyBjörn*. If I put him in the stroller, the screaming was immediate.

It was as if Daniel was a part of me. He felt safe if he was somehow connected to me. I chalked a lot of it up to age-appropriate separation anxiety except it was a bit more than that. But because he was my first child, I had nothing to compare Daniel to other than this group of ten babies. Each child was unique and developed at a difference pace, so I figured I could wait and I really had nothing to worry about.

While these moms were good companions, I have also been very lucky to have Greg as my partner on this journey. The divorce rate among parents of special needs children is unbelievably high. The divorce rate for those without special needs children is very high as it is, but statistically, having a child with needs makes staying married harder. I have seen this statistic play out over and over among people I know.

Some of my friends struggle because one parent believes their child has significant special needs while the other parent is in denial and refuses to see the issues. Some parents fail to see the purpose of therapy and struggle with why the child has to be so scheduled. Some parents feel the child will "grow out of it" and "it's all a phase." It's hard to agree to disagree about your child, especially with the weight of fear, anxiety, and uncertainty circling about.

I felt Greg and I were generally in agreement, and when we decided to renovate our home when Daniel was about four years old, our conversations solidified my confidence in our relationship. In our neighborhood, multiple homes were being renovated. One by one, after each home renovation, the couples were separating and getting divorced. When we decided to do an addition to our home, I said in jest, but not really, "Greg, I love our family first. Our home can be whatever. I'm not renovating if it's going to end up in us splitting."

Without even a pause, Greg said, "Kur, if we can make it work with an interracial, interfaith marriage, with two kids and one child on the spectrum, a little house renovation will not take us down." I have held him to this comment.

We survived the tumultuous home renovation, which put us in an apartment for nine months. During this time, thieves ripped copper from our walls, a new door was stolen from the site, schedules were delayed, a pair of my diamond earrings were burgled, and so many other bizarre happenings occurred one after another. But we made it through and are still living in the house together, married, and loving all the changes we made.

Greg is a terrific and supportive dad, and our common goal to raise both of our children as kind and caring human beings as well as successful members of society has made this journey easier. That said, our younger son Seth and Greg are not mentioned much in this story as this book is more about my experiences with Daniel. But know they are always around volunteering their support and their two cents.

As the mother of a child who is on the high-functioning end of the autism spectrum, I just want my son to be happy. I think all parents want that for their children. So to the other parents raising children who are on the spectrum, I want you to know you are not alone. Even as your story is different from ours, we have similarities in our love for our children, our determination to help and see them overcome every obstacle, and our ability to face our own frustrations and struggles while always showing up. To those just joining the conversation, welcome. You're very important to this conversation, too. Let's keep talking. Invite others. This is the way to raise awareness and create an environment of inclusion.

CHAPTER 2

SURROUNDED BY NOISE

When Daniel was about eighteen months old, a pediatrician I know called and we chatted about our babies. Her daughter is about six months older than Daniel. She talked about how her daughter was having a hard time napping. I commiserated and mentioned that while Daniel did not have issues napping, he did not seem to be pointing at things that caught his interest like the other kids. She hesitated a second and asked for more information. I shared that he didn't really answer to his name, and he had more separation anxiety than the other kids. A few weeks later, she called me and told me she was concerned, and I might want to get Daniel checked out.

I knew in my heart she was right. I could see the differences, but I was hoping she'd say something like, "Pointing is not a big deal and he will probably just start soon," or, "Not answering to his name? That's nothing. All the kids have trouble." I didn't want to know what it was, but I knew something was going on with Daniel.

Soon after, I had Daniel examined. An autism study was looking for infants at the National Institutes of Health, so I signed him up and took him to their offices. The doctors played with him, having him try to pretend play, handle objects, and other fun activities. After that assessment, the doctor said Daniel was not eligible for the study but diagnosed him with PDD-NOS, which stands for Pervasive Developmental Delay, Not Otherwise Specified.

I look back now and wonder why Daniel didn't qualify for the study. Maybe they were looking for more severe cases because, at that point and since, Daniel has always been a high-functioning child on the spectrum. However, this gave me the excuse I needed to continue being in denial about Daniel being on the spectrum at all. I had basically convinced myself that Daniel was delayed and nothing else. Autism, to me, was too scary a concept. It was unknown.

It didn't really matter what he was called—PDD-NOS or autistic. He still had issues, and we were still dealing with them. With this diagnosis, we got him set up with a developmental pediatrician. He told us to apply to Infants and Toddlers—a county program that helps children who are delayed with in-home therapy. I struggled with this task. Applying to this program meant filling out the county forms. I would have to write out on paper and see in black and white the concerns I was having. Something about filling out forms makes medical conditions "official." After procrastinating and then hesitating, hemming and hawing, I finally put on a brave face and decided I had to do it. I filled out the forms and listed Daniel's deficits and weaknesses. We were accepted into the program.

The developmental pediatrician and the Infants and Toddlers program recommended that we take Daniel for a myriad of tests to eliminate any official cause. He had a brain scan that showed he was not prone to seizures. Check. We took him for a hearing test. He had perfect hearing. Check. Vision, fine. Check. So, what was causing all these differences in our son?

It took me a long time to stop worrying about the cause. I played the blame game with myself over and over. Maybe it was because I got food poisoning in my third trimester. Maybe I hugged him too hard. Maybe he was born on a Tuesday and not a Thursday. I've had to let that go. I've had to learn to remind myself the cause doesn't really matter anymore. What's most important is how we try to adapt, and help Daniel adapt, to the differences and challenges. It was more important to move forward rather than backward because life was moving forward, and we had to charge ahead. Some people believe immunizations caused their child's autism. Others believe it's hereditary. I can't get into all of that because this is time and energy I need to spend figuring out how to raise this adorable baby of mine in a world where he mostly fits in but not quite.

One of Daniel's quirks was his ability to tune out the universe when he was playing with a toy, especially one that lit up or played music. He could be engrossed with that toy for twenty to thirty minutes, which is unheard of for a toddler. My friends used to be so impressed at Daniel's ability to sit and play with this one toy we carried with us everywhere we went. The book-shaped toy played songs when different pictures were touched.

The PACE moms and I would go out to lunch and catch up. We all brought our restaurant toys to entertain our kids. Other moms had coloring books, bubbles, stickers, blocks, toys, and more toys. I'd just bring this one song player book. As long as Daniel had that specific music toy, he would sit in the restaurant quietly. He never bothered me as long as he was in my lap or I was sitting next to his highchair. And he never tried to interact with the other kids. The other kids would throw cups on the floor, try to climb under the tables, or get out of their highchairs. Some would try to eat their mom's food or get her attention. But not Daniel. He was happy to be sitting there playing with that toy.

I remember thinking how lucky I was that I could have a conversation and eat my full meal without having to chase my child around a restaurant or constantly pick up a fallen sippy cup. I was thrilled with having a child with such focus that he could tune out the world. I had no idea that I would soon want him to be interacting more with me and the other children. I didn't know this was not a sometimes behavior but a most-of-the-time behavior.

Another favorite toy of Daniel's was the Mozart Cube. I still give this as a gift when friends have babies. The toy is really neat, especially if you are a classical music fan. It is a cube with a large button on all six sides. Each side plays different layers of a piece of music. One side will play the melody, the other will add chords, the other will add the harmony, etc. If you push a side of the cube, it will add that layer of the piece to the song. If all six sides have been pressed, the piece will be played by all sections, and you can add or remove each layer by pushing the corresponding side. Daniel adored this toy. I would put him in the Pack 'n Play with the cube and do whatever I needed to do—cook dinner, do laundry, or even walk out of the room for a bit because he was safe and completely enthralled. As long as I heard the cube playing its music, I knew he was totally fine.

We knew from his choice of toys that Daniel was very musical. His speech was delayed, and he was having difficulty putting words together, but he could hum a tune or fill in notes if I stopped in the middle of a song and waited for him. This was one of our party tricks.

He started picking out notes on the piano around this time. He didn't have the best dexterity, so he would play with his hands instead of individual fingers. He made up pieces and would play them. We used to call them his early compositions. Since I played the piano my whole life, Daniel and I spent many wordless hours sitting in front of the piano playing all kinds of games with the musical notes. Admittedly, these parlor tricks were very cool, and I am guilty of showing them off to friends. I would have given it all up to see Daniel string a sentence together.

Daniel has a language processing disorder. I have decided this is just a fancy way of saying that even if he knew the individual words, putting them together made them meaningless. I doubt that is the official definition of the disorder, but this is how it played out in our house. All of these oddities were a mystery to me.

Most people say when a child is two, they should be stringing two words together. "Mama get," or, "Do it." Daniel's speech delay was interesting. I learned Daniel was able to finish phrases just like he would finish songs I would hum. But he did not seem able to answer questions or talk to me like his peers. I could say, "A dog says…" and he would say, "Woof, woof." But if I said, "What does a dog say?" he would not answer, "Woof, woof." I could point to a color and say, "This circle is…" and he'd say, "Red." But if I pointed to the color red on a color wheel and said, "What color is this?" he would not answer, "Red."

As a stay-at-home mom, I spent a lot of time with Daniel, and we figured out our own way of communicating. Instead of asking questions, I'd make statements. I would model what he *should* say in place of what he *did* say. Every day was a speech lesson. I was also teaching him Japanese at the time but quickly dropped it because it was easier to focus on just English.

Daniel had another speech quirk where he'd repeat what I said. If he wanted me to pick him up, he'd say, "Pick you up. Pick you up," instead of, "Mama, pick me up." I got so used to it I started to not realize it when he said it. He'd also say things like, "You wanna go see friends?" or, "You eat."

I thought he was a mini-genius. I'd read him Dr. Seuss's *ABC* (Seuss, 1963) and Daniel would recite it back. "Big A, little a, what begins with A? Aunt Annie's Alligator, A, A, A." I still remember Daniel reciting the entire book. I thought it was incredible. I figured his speech was coming along fine because just listen to all the words he could say! He could even recite entire books. What I didn't realize was he wasn't *talking*. He wasn't using his own words to create sentences.

I learned what Daniel was doing was called echolalia. He repeated what he heard and used the whole phrase rather than individual words. Since we were communicating and had our little reading games, I didn't really think it was a problem until I learned this was a form of speech delay. We had to get him to make his own sentences and use his own words. It appeared that Daniel was learning whole phrases at a time and using them as words. He did not realize that the words could be separated and used in other ways. I never knew this was a thing.

Once we were accepted into the county Infants and Toddlers program, the therapists came to our house multiple days a week. The various therapists working with Daniel told me he didn't have joint attention. Joint attention is when more than one person looks at or interacts with the same thing. Most kids want a friend or an adult to look at the toy they have in hand or show them an object they find interesting. Daniel had not shown any interest in this. He was unable to use a straw, unable to point, and he didn't really know how to pretend play. We had so much stuff to work on.

For the joint attention concern, I would have to take him outside or around the house and show things I wanted him to look at with me. I'd say, "Look, Daniel, a plane!" with a super excited tone. Then I would put my finger in front of his eyes and make him move his eyes with my finger toward the sky. Then, there was much celebrating over the both of us staring at the sky. Often, he was not very interested in the things I pointed out, and I looked a bit insane. I must have looked quite silly to him and to others who may have been around. Good thing this wasn't about me. It was all about Daniel.

To use a straw, we would light candles or matches and have him practice blowing them out. We would have fake birthday parties and sing happy birthday and then have him try to blow out the flames. For the pretend play, I would sit with Daniel for hours trying to get him to play with toy farmers, blocks, or other items.

To say we had a plethora of toys for these lessons is an understatement. These were not simply toys in our house. They pretty much all served some sort of educational purpose. It was every day, all day.

One thing I remember doing, which I thought was kind of mean, was to make things harder for Daniel to reach so he would have to ask for them. For example, if he wanted a favorite toy, like a plastic cowboy, I'd have to put it higher on a shelf so Daniel would have to ask, "Mama, can I have that toy?" I know it was to get him talking, but I always felt bad about it.

All of this play therapy and candle blowing happened right around the time Daniel turned two and Seth was born. In retrospect, I am glad this all happened in the haze of having a second child because, with each new report I read, it was clearer Daniel was not like other kids. But instead of spiraling out of control, I was just doing my best to get two kids dressed, fed, and entertained every day. In my opinion, even today, nothing is worse than seeing the deficits of one's child in writing. Having to discuss it further is another form of nausea-inducing uncomfortableness.

The signs were everywhere. It was impossible to stay oblivious and in denial. During music classes, Daniel was spinning in the corner while everyone else was in a circle rolling balls back and forth to the teacher. In gym class, everyone would be following the leader and Daniel was making piles of bean bags in the corner over and over. In gymnastics, all the kids were running around and jumping, but Daniel clung to me while sitting on my lap. With these obvious signs and the written reports by our therapists, it became clear Daniel needed extra help. So we got him help.

We put together Team Daniel with a developmental pediatrician. He recommended we get him verbal behavior therapy forty hours a week. He also recommended Daniel attend classes and be in social environments with typical children as role models. Since we had graduated the free in-home therapy program offered by the county, we put Daniel in the early preschool program at a nearby elementary school a few days a week. This program was also offered by the county. On the other days, we enrolled him in swimming, soccer, piano, art, acting, music classes, and more. At three years old, Daniel was the busiest preschool child in the neighborhood. When he was not in the county preschool, he was at his private preschool where we hired a therapist to shadow him and encourage him to use his words and interact with other students. Then, he would come home and spend the afternoon with the same or a different therapist using the Verbal Behavior program in addition to his activities.

Verbal Behavior mixed memorizing and flashcard drills with play-based learning. He would have some table time, and then Daniel would work toward a reward of three minutes of play with a favorite toy. I thought this was doable, and the therapists had a way of tracking progress. We had binders of reports, charts, successes, and areas of improvement. I liked that we had a way to track progress. Daniel liked it because the therapists were always bringing new and enticingly fun toys for him to explore, mostly with music and flashing lights. If I am being truly honest here, I was also very glad to have the brunt of the play therapy taken over by the professionals as I was getting pretty run down and did not know exactly what I was doing.

I was, however, kept quite busy with homework, as I called it. The Verbal Behavior therapy relied on flashcards that had to be created—boxes of them. We also had to take photographs. I would have lists of things to photograph so Daniel could improve his vocabulary. I would take pictures of his clothing, his school, the supermarket, the teachers, food items, store clerks, the store signs, you name it. The photos were printed at CVS and brought back for me to create notecards. I was the only mom of a toddler and an infant not attending school to have homework to do. The more I did this kind of work, the more I felt like I was making a tangible difference in his speech therapy. But sometimes, I wished it was just easier.

Once Daniel had forty hours of fun-based learning supervised by professionals, Greg and I had some time back for ourselves—time to focus on our worries. We were spiraling down a dark anxiety tunnel. We were concerned about his future because we didn't know what it would look like for a kid like him. I remember Greg asking one of our therapists, "Do you think I'll ever be able to have a conversation with my son?" Our Verbal Behavior therapist assured us this would be possible. I was a bit dubious, but I still clung to this comment. I would tell myself all the time, "One day, I will be able to have a conversation with my son."

Watching Daniel learn how to talk was interesting. Most children learn things naturally. Like nodding yes and shaking their head no. They see it enough times, put it all in context, and soon they are using words or shaking their heads. Learning concepts like me/mine, you/yours, even answering questions is natural. With Daniel, each of these things had to be broken down and taught little by little, mostly by the verbal behavior teachers and our family. I wanted to turn that switch on in the language processing section of Daniel's brain so he, too, could learn by watching and through social experience, not over a table with therapists and flashcards.

I thought about this a lot. No one really remembers learning how to talk. We were too young. We just know we learned it at some point. I guess it is more like when you learn a second language that you start to think about how language is processed.

When I was first living in America, and I was trying to learn how to speak English, I remember how complicated it was. The English as a Second Language teachers were speaking to me in English, which I did not understand, to try to teach me English, which I did not speak. At five, I did not grasp the concept that English was a language. I remember sort of cruising through my early days of kindergarten just watching the clock and hearing the noise of it all. What was worse was that all the kids had these strange names and I couldn't remember them. They would say their names, Michelle, Christina, or Laura. But these sounds were so foreign to me I knew I would never be able to say them. It is hard to make friends when you can't even remember or pronounce the other person's name. I feel like we take these things for granted.

My brother, my mom, and I would laugh over dinner about how strange English was and how everything sounded so different. People would walk us around saying, "I'll show you this," or, "I'll show you that," but all we heard was "oshouyu" this "oshouyu" that. *Oshouyu* is Japanese for soy sauce. How peculiar these people were, soy sauce this and soy sauce that.

I remember my brother coming home quite frustrated and my mom asking what happened. My brother reported that he was walked to the bathroom multiple times that day. He explained that if he knew the answer to a problem, he decided to raise his hand and answer in Japanese. Apparently, the teachers thought he was asking to be taken to the bathroom, so they would instruct the kind friends he was making in class to take him there, repeatedly. As individual stories, these are all comical. But if this happened to you over and over, day after day, imagine how overwhelming it would be.

One day, a teacher put a piece of paper in front of me with a line drawing of a foot. The toe section was circled, and the teacher pointed to it over and over saying, "Toe. This is a toe. Toe here. This is a toe." In that moment, it occurred to me the word or sound she was making for the big toe actually meant toe. This was an "aha" moment for me and exactly when I realized that for every Japanese word I knew, there was a parallel English word. Toe meant *ashiyubi*. All I had to do was learn the English counterparts to my Japanese vocabulary, and I would be able to understand these teachers.

Once I started to hear individual words from English speakers, and not just noise, I became fluent very quickly. I believe I graduated ESL the year after I arrived at school and was mainstreamed into the classroom.

But even this isn't exactly the same as Daniel's experience learning how to speak. I already had a language to match the words. He did not have that fundamental layer.

I think for many years, Daniel was surrounded by noise.

CHAPTER 3

CAN'T FIND IT? CREATE IT.

Daniel eventually did start speaking. He was making his way out of the sounds and noise and hearing individual words. The therapy was helping, and I realized my son had a remarkable strength of being teachable. Once language was broken up, explained, and taught repeatedly, Daniel started to master words.

But Daniel did not respond to his name. I often feared going places with Daniel because I knew that if we let go of each other I might never find him again due to this simple problem. This was an issue in the store if he got ahead of me or turned a corner. I would call for him, "Daniel, where are you, bud?" But I was met with silence. Daniel was not used to responding to his name. So we started the "Daniel, what Daniel." Whenever I said his name, I would say "Daniel, what Daniel," so he would remember that phrase. Once that was in place and securely registered as a phrase in his mind, if I only said, "Daniel," the phrase was unfinished. This prompted Daniel to respond with, "What Daniel," and then eventually, just, "What."

Daniel also loved to sing songs, so whenever I needed to get him motivated, I would make up a song. Somehow singing about bath time was much more acceptable than telling him it was bath time. I made up songs about everything and we still remember some of them now. I had one song about the names of the cousins, but that one had to keep changing as he kept gaining cousins year after year. My proudest piece was my cell phone number. I turned that into a little jingle that stuck, and both the boys will hum the tune when they have to tell someone my contact info. They have since dropped the jazz hands move in the end with the "yeah!" I had taught them.

Realizing that teaching him little tricks and cues like this did not take long to master, I was starting to see how much he could learn if I taught him in a way he learned. Daniel is pretty rigid and likes rules. If I could play on those rules, I could achieve success.

The problem was that I did not always know how to teach him. The therapists also had many lessons that worked. The flashcards with the pictures were very clever. The play therapy was also successful. Having Daniel use words like "over" and "under" and then having him physically go over and under something, labeling while doing it and then seeing it in a book, helped him. All of these repetitive actions helped him generalize vocabulary and concepts.

Similarly, we spent a while teaching him the names of the rooms in our house. I would be in one place in the house and tell him to "go to the dining room." He knew where the rooms were in our house, but he did not know each had a name, something most kids learn without being taught and or when just told once. I would say, "Go to the dining room," and when he got there, I'd give him praise. Then the next room, and the next room, until he knew the names of each of the rooms in the house.

Then it was time to work on multistep directions. We would say, "Go to the dining room, get the book on the table, and put it in the kitchen next to Dad." This seemingly easy task assumes the child knows what a book is, what "on a table" is, what the various rooms are, the direction of taking a book and moving it into the other room, and knowing what "next to" meant, all after hearing it once. During a period of time, I had Daniel running around doing meaningless tasks just to reinforce the names of the rooms and practicing multistep directions. The rest of the family thought nothing of Daniel handing them things or picking up things from room to room and carried on with their activities.

As teachable as Daniel was in those days, words and fluency were slow to come. How frustrating it must have been to want to say something but not know the order of the words or enough words to say it. How frustrating it must have been not understanding requests from people and having them think you were obstinate or a bad listener rather than simply confused. I think these are some of the reasons we had frequent outbursts and tantrums during this time.

My first summer living in the United States, my parents signed me up for summer camp at the local YMCA, mostly so we would have something to do during the day. I was with a group of kids all going into the first grade. I was still not exactly fluent in English. I knew some things in English, but it was clearly still my second language, and I needed more practice and confidence to speak the words out loud.

One day, in between activities, I had to use the restroom, so I joined a group of girls going in that direction. In Japan, most children carry a handkerchief so they can dry their hands. But

I stopped carrying one because I was now in America. After washing my hands and realizing the paper towels were out, I wiped my hands on the back of my shorts. When I came out of the bathroom, one of the girls in my group wacked my behind for reasons I will never know. When she realized my shorts were wet, she started chanting, "Kuri peed her pants!"

I wanted to say, "No! I just wiped my hands!" But I was frozen. I only knew how to say these words in Japanese. I was letting this girl chant nonsense about me, and I was not happy about it. The level of frustration rising in me was so high I still remember that feeling today.

This is the kind of frustration I knew Daniel was feeling every time he was tripping over his words in the beginning of mastering language processing. When I was levelheaded, I could appreciate his emotions and would be understanding. But not when I was not levelheaded. It is hard to stay calm when parenting a child who is exploding for no apparent reason. I'm sure he always had a reason, but sometimes I didn't see it.

Luckily for me that day at the YMCA, a girl I knew from my elementary school was there, and she stuck up for me. I remember her saying, "No, she just wiped her hands," and gesturing me to get moving, ending that awful scene. I still remember, and I thank her for that rescue.

Kids are random and do things they don't think will make such a lasting impression. I will never forget the chanting or the relief I felt when someone spoke the words for me. I have always tried to pay it forward and speak for the person who can't get the words out. If Daniel can't say it, I will. If someone else is struggling, I will try to help that person.

As Daniel got older, I noticed I had a hard time finding places where I felt comfortable dropping him off. For me, I wouldn't even consider a camp, activity, or class that did not have teachers and counselors who knew how to interact with kids with speech delays and a bit of crying. I wanted to make sure someone there was willing and, more importantly, wanting to help Daniel if he needed it. As part of the directives from Team Daniel, putting him in out-of-school activities was very important to experience social skills and learn how to interact with children and adults, but a few negative experiences made me a bit anxious.

One such experience was with a substitute piano teacher. Daniel had shown immediate interest and skills in music. Growing up, I played the piano, and we always had a piano in our house. My parents bought the piano we have in our house today when we first moved to the United States. I started to teach Daniel how to play a few songs and he took to it very quickly. I decided to find him a piano teacher because knowing how to play the piano does not mean you can successfully teach your son how to play.

We tried all sorts of teachers. One program I liked sent teachers to the home. This allowed me to help smooth things out when Daniel didn't understand the teacher or the teacher didn't understand Daniel.

Unfortunately, every time we got comfortable with a teacher, they would move away or get a different gig and stop teaching. I decided to find a Suzuki teacher because it was clear that Daniel had perfect pitch. This meant he could hear notes and know what they were without looking to see what was played. He could pick up songs and play them back by ear. The Suzuki method teaches music by listening to it not by reading the notes. I thought it was a great idea because Daniel was too young to read anyway, and it was also the way I learned how to play the piano.

My great idea was a bust because the only Suzuki program I found locally wanted Daniel to silently observe a lesson a few times before enrolling him. This was not such an easy feat as Daniel was about three years old and wouldn't sit still or quietly to watch a piano lesson. What three-year-old could? Due to the studio space being rented, the teacher only allowed the children to color or draw using the type of markers that showed up in color on special paper. This was all too much for me. I decided to forgo Suzuki entirely and let go of the dream.

I found a Russian teacher who was "great with young kids" at a music school near our house. She turned out to be the right fit for Daniel. She was patient, had a son similar in age to Daniel, was an incredibly talented piano player, and was okay with Daniel's personality because she saw that he could play the pieces she assigned. And really, that was all that mattered. They got along nicely.

Daniel and the teacher figured out a way to work with each other, and he was steadily improving. I was impressed and relieved that the responsibility of giving him the skills to get into Julliard was now transferred to someone else more capable.

One day, quite unexpectedly, our teacher was out for the week. We didn't know until we arrived at the lesson and saw a substitute teacher. About ten minutes into the lesson, the substitute teacher stormed out of the small private room into the waiting room where I was playing with Seth.

"This child is not teachable!" she ranted. She then pointed to her next student. "See that boy? He is young like your child, but *he* listens."

I was furious, not only at what she said, but that she was ranting and raving in front of other children and parents.

As much as I wanted to deck this woman, I had to model good behavior for my own children. I was so angry I did not have any space left in me to feel embarrassed at the scene she was causing. I told her we were done for the day and left carrying one kid and holding my other child's hand. Daniel seemed unfazed by the drama he inadvertently created. He was probably glad the lesson got cut short.

Later, I wrote a letter to the music school. I put in detail how she created a scene in the waiting room rather than pulling me aside and talking to me privately. I included my thoughts about how a teacher should have the skills to teach a child instead of blaming my son for not having instructional control of the situation. She knew I was sitting in the waiting room, and she never came out to ask me if I could help or intervene. The school agreed to never have her substitute for Daniel again. If his regular teacher was sick, Daniel could skip that lesson, free of charge, rather than being taught by a different teacher.

Another negative experience was when I put Daniel in his first acting camp in second grade. I had a gut feeling it was not going to be successful, but I couldn't find another camp that fit our schedule. It was a reputable camp, so I signed Daniel up. I had a call with the director to explain that Daniel was on the autism spectrum, had a hard time with social skills and language skills, and would need a little extra attention.

A few days into the program, the same director told me Daniel had been unfocused and was trying to get attention by acting out. She said her staff was having to spend too much time directing and redirecting Daniel. I was a bit surprised as she and I had discussed his need for extra attention on the call. I told her I would talk with Daniel and encourage him to be less disruptive. I also decided to drop him off later in the morning and pick him up a few hours earlier so I could observe and keep him from disrupting the program.

From my chat with Daniel and my observations, I saw that the camp was very loosely structured. The play was created and written by the kids. The set was being created by the kids. The counselors were there to assist the production and to rehearse the lines and songs. The majority of the kids were a few years older than Daniel. Daniel was given one line to sing in the whole production. While the other campers were busy learning lines and creating sets, Daniel had nothing to do. He was clearly lost without any direction being given.

Later in the week, I walked in with Daniel hand in hand. As we walked into the main area, I saw one counselor roll her eyes and look to another colleague as if to say, "Look who's back." I wanted to pull Daniel right then and there, but Daniel was so excited for the performance at the end of the session. I also could not think of a good explanation to give Daniel for pulling him from the camp so abruptly. I gritted my teeth, dropped off Daniel, and again explained to the counselor that he needed to be assigned an activity during down time and that unstructured time was a problem for him. I gave suggestions so Daniel would have a specific activity to be engaged in and would not need to act out because of being bored. Luckily, the two-week camp was almost over at this point. I continued to pick him up a few hours early every day and left without making any eye contact with the adults.

Happily, the performance was a great success. Daniel nailed his one line as he sang his eight-second solo. He sang in tune, on time, and he came in on cue. Greg and I were very proud of his performance, clapped very loudly, cheered his name, and walked out of that space. Daniel felt he accomplished something, and he had! Most importantly, he was very happy.

I swore I would never ever darken that camp doorway again. For a moment, I considered talking to the head of the program to explain what would help if she had students similar to Daniel in the future, but I didn't. I did not feel gracious enough to educate her so she could improve her program. I was hurt and mad, and I could not get past it at that time. It's not really my job to make all places better. Sometimes I do take the extra time and try to do so, but some people don't want to hear my words and some people won't benefit from them. So, I walked on, and I think that's okay.

I have since let it go. I sometimes wonder if I was not as clear as I needed to be about the extra attention I thought Daniel would need. Perhaps I wanted the camp to work out so much that I ignored the fact it was geared toward older children who needed less direction. I learned I should listen to my gut. And, after this experience, I always have. If I get a feeling the instructors or counselors are not qualified, I do not use that program. Even if the counselors are qualified, if I don't see they are interested in working with children like Daniel, I look for a different option.

After having a few of these interactions and learning that not every teacher has the knowledge to teach children like Daniel, I decided it was easier to set up my own programs.

I put together my own soccer teams and practices with companies that let you create your own groups if you have a certain minimum number of students. Once there was a set number of participants, the company would give you a coach and schedule a field. It was a little extra work on my part, sending emails to the class list and finding kids who would join, but it was definitely worth it.

I could find the right coach for the kids. I would generally ask for a person who was extra skilled with children or who was most open to trying new ideas. I would pull the coach aside and share the quirks about Daniel that could come up during practice and give a quick list of helpful hints. Perhaps Daniel would not sit on the grass like the other kids, but he would sit on a jacket or a ball. Perhaps he would not understand the directions for passing a ball back and forth. But if he was third or fourth in line to do the exercise, he could watch and see what was expected. Some of these tips were beneficial to other kids in the group, not just Daniel. The more control over the class I had, the more I could relax, knowing Daniel would not be treated differently. I wouldn't have to worry.

I was also the snack queen. Nothing makes parents and kids happier than someone who shows up every week with a huge container of coffee from Starbucks and a basket full of bananas and clementine oranges. Parents generally had to stay and watch during the practices. I knew the happier the parents were, and the smoother the activities went, the more likely they would sign on for more and more seasons.

Some programs in our area excelled in working with children on the spectrum. They would provide extra support and staff with special education training to help make the program a success for all the children.

As part of developing Daniel's social skills, we always had a goal to place Daniel in environments where he could interact with typical children and watch their modeled behavior. Finding such programs that would accept him was trickier, but these programs became more and more available as Daniel got older. Around third grade, I was able to find more programs that provided inclusion, and most of them were very fun and positive. I found small local groups that would go out of their way to accommodate us.

One of the programs I felt very comfortable taking both my boys to was a local baseball camp. The first day, I pulled the counselor aside and explained how Daniel had some trouble with language comprehension. I told him baseball may not be Daniel's favorite activity, that he was not interested in getting too hot, and he didn't really know how to interact with others that well. This coach, who was probably in high school, looked me straight in the eye and said, "No problem. I will make sure he has a good day." He seemed to mean it. He was young, enthusiastic, and very friendly, so I knew that if Daniel didn't take to the baseball part of the camp, he would at least like his counselor.

It was a half-day camp and I was back to pick up both kids within a few hours. When I got there, the counselor said to me, "I was a lot like Daniel when I was younger. And he was fun. I hope he comes back tomorrow." The young man probably never thought about that comment again after we waved goodbye. I, however, played it over and over in my head. It made me so happy to hear that my son was a joy.

Hearing that the counselor had also been like my son when he was younger made such an impression on me. I had no idea how Daniel would turn out when he was older, so hearing that this nice young man had been similar to Daniel was a relief. I wrote a note to the head of the camp thanking them for the great experience, and I called out that counselor for his kindness.

This is also something I do often. When I see someone who goes out of his or her way to be extra thoughtful, I send a note to the person's boss. I do this because that is something to be noted.

Although Daniel did not end up picking baseball as his favorite activity, he has continued to play the piano and has way surpassed me and my skills. Daniel continues to love acting and performing in plays and has landed some great roles as Mr. Warbucks in *Annie*, King Triton in *Little Mermaid*, and the lead as Beast in *Beauty and the Beast*. It is amazing to watch Daniel perform on stage and exude such joy.

CHAPTER 4

SWIM! SWIM! SWIM!

With a few years of preschool (public and private), a variety of extracurricular activities, speech therapy, and social skills classes under our belt, it was time to look for an elementary school for Daniel. At five years old and at this point of his development, Daniel was a happy boy who loved music, was skilled at playing the piano, and had language processing issues along with a speech delay. He had a hard time being in sync with his peers, but he was happy to play near them. He was great at group activities with a leader, but he mostly preferred to play alone.

With Daniel's mid-August birthday, Greg and I had to decide if we should push him into kindergarten, or should we hold him back a year. What was the right thing to do? When Daniel was a baby, someone gave me some unsolicited advice that having a baby in August was tricky because of the placement decision. But she said by the time we'd have to decide these things, we'd just know. I was dubious but kept it in mind. When I toured the public school's kindergarten program, I knew in my gut that Daniel was not ready. He needed an extra year.

During that extra year, I studied the private and public options available. I visited Montessori school programs, small private schools, big private schools, progressive schools, and some schools for children with learning disabilities. I wanted to know what was out there and where he would best fit. I wanted a school that *wanted* to teach and work with him *because* of his quirks, not despite his quirks.

In our area, we were very fortunate to have a variety of schools to choose from and more schools being developed frequently. Our public schools are very respected, and people move into our county to attend them. The area's private schools are also highly desirable, and many have an arduous application process with limited spots. The public school sounded like a possible option, but I knew the class size was large and our specialists recommended a small class size to optimize Daniel's learning. The public school was about to be under construction, and I was worried Daniel would not do well with the transitions. I narrowed the search to private schools with small classes and teachers trained to work with children with special needs and delays.

After touring many different programs in the area, the school I most wanted to enroll Daniel in was called The Maddux School. It was a newer private school at the time. They had twelve to fifteen kids per class, and each child had some sort of social skills deficit. All classes had two teachers and the lead teachers had degrees in special education. Speech therapists and occupational therapists were on staff working with all of the students.

But what won me over happened during the informational interview. The assistant director said, "At Maddux, no child plays alone." One of the key parts of the curriculum was social skills. The school's main goal was for the students to want to interact with each other. The school would break down and teach social skills and social development. The assistant director said, "Children can play alone when they are at home. But at school, they will play with each other and learn how to do so."

It sounded like the ideal environment for my son and the friendliest, nicest place for any child. I had noticed Daniel choosing to play alone rather than seeking out friends, and I was worried he would not be able to make friends or be accepted by others. There is a limit to what a parent can teach. There's even a limit to what a therapist can teach. Sometimes, the only thing that really works is real-time real-life experiences. Fortuitously, this school was offering just that. Once Greg and I took the official school tour together, we decided we had to get Daniel enrolled. I was a woman on a mission. It was Maddux or bust.

I started a letter-writing campaign. I had friends, teachers, and anyone who had anything nice to say about Daniel write a letter to the school. I had friends call friends who had friends at the school to call on our behalf.

I didn't stop there. I wrote on every page of the application how if they accepted Daniel, they would be accepting me, too. I would volunteer to do whatever they needed. Class mom, event organizer, parent volunteer, fieldtrip chaperone—whatever they needed. All they had to do was take Daniel and they got all that help for free.

Living in this area and in this county, I know we are incredibly lucky to have the options that may not be available in all parts of the country. Many schools and private programs cater to children with special needs. I am so grateful for all of the options we had to create Team Daniel. We were also fortunate because I was able to be a stay-at-home mother after Daniel was born, which allowed me to be available to volunteer a significant amount of time. I appreciated this whole heartedly.

After significant stress eating along with anxious days and weeks and months of waiting, we finally heard back from the school. Daniel was accepted into their Pre-K program! I burst into tears of joy.

I did not flake on the things I offered. I ran fall harvest festivals and came in any time they needed a parent for sharing days. I visited Daniel's class every year during the holidays with a borrowed keyboard and played our favorite game of "name that tune" with seasonal songs. I brought books and stories about Japan and talked about my culture. I won Daniel's classmates over by bringing in a Japanese Power Rangers book and telling them these mighty morphing heroes originated in Japan. Japanese snacks also helped. I even volunteered to sing the Hebrew prayers and light the Chanukah candles for the winter lights ceremony. I kept my word and then some.

Daniel flourished at Maddux. I was able to relax a bit, knowing professionals were now teaching Daniel all the social and coping skills he really needed. It was nice to know Daniel was in a class filled with kids who also needed a little extra help and he was not alone.

At Maddux, Daniel went from a tiny preschooler who walked around clutching a printed visual calendar of the day to manage his anxiety to a proud second grader who had playdates, went to movies with his classmates, and performed in piano recitals twice a year.

Much later, Daniel told me he did not understand what the teachers were saying the first two years of starting school. This made me think of when I first came to America and was in kindergarten. I arrived in December and in the spring, we had an Easter celebration. Growing up in Japan, where Christianity is not common, I had no concept of Easter. I remember coming back from a specials class, like art or music, and the classroom was decorated with eggs and rabbits. More confusion. Then, the teacher handed me a piece of paper on which were drawn some rectangles and dots. I was to understand that these rectangles were the desks and these dots were eggs that had been hidden.

I remember when I got home telling my mom about the utter confusion I experienced at school as we sipped tea and snacked. Why in the world would I want to find eggs? When I showed her they opened, and they had little candy chocolate eggs inside, we were both just flabbergasted. The Easter Bunny and an Easter egg hunt were so out of my realm of reality that for a moment, I thought I had entered The Twilight Zone.

Only years later did I understand what the mad dash for those plastic colorful eggs meant. I think Daniel had similar experiences in his early school days when he did not understand what the teachers were saying. He probably sat there knowing things were happening around him but just not really understanding why and, more importantly, what his role was in the bustle of activity.

At his new school, Daniel and I both made friends. We still see them a few times a year. We call his peers the Maddux friends, and mine are the Maddux moms. Back then, on days off from school, the parents would organize a day at the park and all the kids would get together and run around. These unstructured times were more successful because they had been practicing how to play with each other at school recess. On half days from school, the moms would take all the kids to a nearby restaurant and let the kids sit together and socialize. I couldn't believe the growth I saw as Daniel chatted with his peers.

Daniel was learning more than academics at school. He was learning self-regulation, labeling different moods, self-advocacy, and social skills. He was a model student. He never got in trouble, was always sweet, and never broke the rules. This kind of behavior is not very easy to maintain throughout the day. He was great at school for his teachers, but at home, he would be so tired from trying to be good all day that he would inevitably fall apart. It was really hard trying to parent a child who was exhausted from being good all day and was about to lose it as soon as he walked in the door.

I was assured that the positive side to this was that "Daniel knows *how* to behave well," and "Daniel has recognized multiple environments and can adjust his behavior accordingly." I was also told that he had no qualms about acting out at home because he knew that we, his family, would love him no matter what. Daniel understood this might not be the case in an environment like school. These facts were not as comforting as they were intended to be while I was in the thick of it at home after school.

At that point, we hired new therapists in addition to the speech therapists to help work on behavior issues. Daniel hated the word no. It was his way or the highway. He hated when we had to do things he didn't like. He didn't like to try new things. He didn't want to go to new places. He didn't want to turn off the TV. He didn't want me to tell him when to get in the bath. He did not like a lot of things.

It's hard to put a child in therapy when he is so young. First, the language delay and processing make it hard to know if either side is understanding the other. Is Daniel expressing his concerns in a way the therapist understands? Is Daniel understanding the suggestions made by the therapists? How can talking with a therapist teach you to manage your impulse control? Could I be told not to be impulsive and comply? Does a visual chart really make me go get a glass of water when I am angry? Or will I decide to rage instead and then wish I had gotten that glass of water?

Daniel and Seth used to take swim lessons at the local Jewish Community Center. I was adamant that both boys learn how to swim and tread water as a safety issue. During their lessons, other lessons were happening in the adjacent lanes. Every week, there was a boy who was being coached by an older male swim coach. I'm sure he taught the child how to blow bubbles and the basics with the kickboards like my kids were learning, but we all remember him shouting at the kid in the pool, "Swim! Swim! Swim!"

This became an ongoing joke in our house. Whenever I wanted Seth to take a nap, I would shout, "Nap! Nap! Nap!" Or when teaching Daniel how to read, I would shout, "Read! Read! Read!" It would be fantastic if I could report that this method was successful, but it was not. It was just funny and would make us crack up every time.

Teaching a new behavior, like reading or swimming, is difficult. But I find that eliminating unwanted behavior is, for me, much harder. When Seth was born, he had a full head of hair. In the very first photo I have of the two boys together, Daniel has his hand on Seth's head. I can look through our albums for years and years, and most of the photos of the two of them show Daniel with his hand on Seth's head. When Seth was an infant, this was not an issue. Until it was.

By the time it was an issue, it was a habit. It was just something Daniel did. So, years into this becoming a daily occurrence, we had to get Daniel to stop doing it. Seth didn't like it, and well, it was just odd. But, when the urge to do it is way stronger and more satisfying than the urge to *not* do it, eliminating the behavior becomes challenging.

Around this time, I tried "attending and commenting." This therapy was intended to minimalize Daniel's negative behaviors and increase his positive ones. I was instructed to comment in a neutral voice on everything my child did and attend to him (pay attention to him). But when he started doing something that was not preferred, or a behavior we wanted to eliminate, I would remove my attending and my commenting.

Just like a sportscaster reporting the events of a game, I would narrate the events of our day. I'd say, "Daniel, I see you're just sitting there, sitting on the floor. Yup, feet in front of you. Breathing. Steady breathing. Good job sitting still and breathing and just being there. Calm. That's how you're feeling. Calm. Breathing. Yup. Still breathing and sitting. Wow. Okay." And on and on and on. If I liked the neutral and calm behavior, I would add in some positive reinforcements because I much preferred neutral to the negative. If Daniel put his hand on Seth's head, I would remove my attention from him wordlessly until he started doing something that was neutral or positive again.

As a result of this method, I am proud to say I can find something positive to say about anything in any situation. Child crying like a maniac? "Wow, you can really make your thoughts known." Child sitting doing nothing? "I love how you can sit there just like that. Not moving." This is one of my superpowers. I can turn anything into positive reinforcement.

Imagine how excited I get if I see actual positive behavior. The cheerleader in me comes out and the praise starts flowing.

I might even throw in a little jump and a split. But I could not really maintain this commenting consistently, so I had to turn to alternate approaches.

Our different doctors and therapists suggested I try many things. I tried them all. The "marble jar method" was a behavior plan that seemed like a good idea in theory. I was told to split the day into chunks—before school, after school until dinner, after dinner until bed time, and bed time, for example. I was to create a list of positive behaviors and a list of negative behaviors. If Daniel presented only the positive behaviors during a period, a marble would be added to the jar. If he exhibited bad behaviors, a marble was taken out of the jar. The goal was to fill the jar with marbles and then Daniel could receive a prize.

When I offered that this sounded a bit like bribing, the therapist said that frankly no one is motivated to do anything without a carrot. "Your husband wouldn't go to work if he didn't earn a salary. Correct?" she said. "And his salary is not considered a bribe. It is earned. It is a reward."

I didn't question it. I just accepted it and pressed onward. In retrospect, perhaps I needed to use a smaller jar—like the baby food-sized ones. I can't tell you how many jars we never filled with this method.

It was all smiles and happy faces when the marbles were added. We would praise him for being a sweet child and following the list of good behaviors to the letter. However, when it was necessary to remove a marble, this was a big trigger for Daniel. He would inevitably do something on the negative behavior list, like put his hand on Seth's head and not remove it when asked. Daniel would then lose a marble. Rather than acknowledging that he blatantly ignored his brother's request, which was the reason he lost a marble, he would be tremendously upset that I would dare take a marble out of the jar. This would send Daniel into a tailspin, which would start a new series of negative behaviors, which resulted in more marbles being removed.

These tirades would usually end with shouting matches and time-outs, which never worked. For a time-out to work, the child would have to stay seated or be in a room for a particular amount of time. What happens when the child is so worked up he won't comply and stay on the step or in the chair? Well, that becomes phase three—the next tantrum.

I would hate it so much that I would not take marbles out of the jar. This would make the whole system moot as the most important thing with these plans is to stay consistent. I was crumbling under the pressure. I did not have the strength to take on the "marble jar."

I watched a friend of mine put her child in a time-out once. The boy misbehaved so my friend told her son to sit by the playground structure (about ten feet from us) for a time-out, and he went. He sat on the step of the structure until he was told to come back. I could not believe what I was watching.

I pretty much broke down after this. How was I such a failure as a parent that I could not get my child to listen to me? Was I too mean? Was I too soft? What was I doing wrong? Every bit of my parenting was challenged. I never imagined discipline could work like this. I sometimes resented spending time with other families because it made me realize how I was failing and others were doing it better. Never mind that my circumstances were different. I was just defeated.

It is so easy to play the comparison game as a parent and as a person. As destructive as it is, I cannot help myself at times. At least social media wasn't so readily available at the time. I am not sure I would have been able to handle an onslaught of happy family posts and videos of cute siblings playing together. I even burst into tears one day when some women were talking about how they went on a family walk with their kids. All I could think of was how I could never do that. I could never get both kids to agree to go for a walk without tremendous pre-planning and effort and these people just up and go. Tears and more tears.

I wish I could be the kind of human who didn't get jealous, who was centered and above all of this. But in truth, I am petty. When my boys were little, I remember listening to a mom telling a story about how her daughter had acted up at the deli. Her daughter was not pleased with something so she took a napkin and threw it on the ground. I was thinking, *And? And then what happened?* What about the part where the mom nicely asks the girl to pick it up, and then the girl goes into a fit and starts yelling for the mom to pick it up, at which point the other people in the store start to look. And then the mom starts to think *Oh no, they think I'm a terrible mom for not being able to control my daughter.* She forcibly removes her daughter and herself from the deli due to the loud scene playing out and has to go to a drive-through with the child safely strapped in the car seat…

I was waiting and waiting. Nope, that was it. The daughter threw a crumpled napkin on the floor. I *wished* that was all my child did.

I used to joke, though not really a funny joke, that my children did not understand the concept of commerce because I refused to take them on outings. They had not been to a supermarket or witnessed a financial exchange because it was just too much for me to leave the house with them. Not knowing what would set off my son was enough to turn me into a hermit, but we pressed on because we had to eventually get to places and attend activities.

We visited multiple therapists and tried many different techniques. Some of them were successful, and some were not. Some failed because I could not stay consistent and maintain the programs. Some behaviors just went away on their own. Other behaviors were phases that were replaced with the next thing and the next thing. I am not sure which therapies worked and which did not, but I know that without them I wouldn't have had one of my favorite memories to date.

Even though it may seem like there was a lot of drama and tantrums, we have also had many laugh-out-loud moments. One afternoon, when Daniel was eight years old, we were in a waiting room. We often sat with the same people every week waiting for the various therapists in the same practice. A very nice man told me that his son, who was much older than Daniel, was also on the autism spectrum and having difficulty adjusting in high school. He was very informative, telling me about the middle school and high school programs available locally.

This man was bald and had a bit of a longish face. Daniel looked straight at the man and said, "Voldemort. Are you Voldemort?"

I was mortified. The man was stunned silent. Daniel was very serious.

After a few long seconds, Voldemort got it together and told Daniel gently that he was not He-Who-Must-Not-Be-Named. He was a dad waiting for his son.

I don't know if Daniel was entirely convinced. Luckily for us, our therapist called us in and I ushered Daniel quickly out of the room. From that point on, we decided to wait in the car until just a few seconds before our sessions. I told Daniel that if he had the urge to vocalize his thoughts about the man being Voldemort again, he should tap his nose with his finger and I would understand. We did a lot of nose tapping until eventually Mr. Voldemort stopped coming or switched appointment times.

I look back at that scene and heartily agree that the dad *did* resemble Voldemort. Daniel, as usual, was spot on with his observations. If we're still playing the comparison game, I admit that my friend's daughter is calmer than my son, and my other friend's son is a better listener. But I completely win in the Daniel-making-me-laugh-out-loud-with-his-truth-bombs category.

CHAPTER 5

TO TELL OR NOT TO TELL

As one of our many therapy goals for Daniel was to work on his gross and fine motor skills and follow multistep directions involving physical movement, Greg and I decided to sign up Daniel and Seth for martial arts. It was perfect timing as Seth was in first grade and wanted to be a superhero/ninja/Power Ranger, and Daniel was starting third grade at a new school close to a martial arts studio. We were at the studio multiple times a week. The studio was set up in a way so the students would work out on the mats and the parents would sit, watch, and wait from the rows of seats.

One afternoon, Daniel came running to me in a fit of rage and said, "That boy hit me! He hit me and he pushed me!"

Accustomed to Daniel's outbursts, I calmly said, "Okay, then just stay away from him."

Nope, this did not work. Daniel was very upset. He went on, "No! You have to go yell at him!"

I responded sternly, "No, I shouldn't have to get involved. You need to work it out with the instructors."

Seth arrived with the report as he is usually the voice of truth in these situations. "Mama, Daniel was following me and copying me and I told him to stop. But he didn't. So that boy told Daniel to stop bothering me and pushed him aside."

Now that I knew the full context of the scenario, I saw Daniel instigated the incident, and I was right in my initial decision that I didn't need to intervene.

The boy who allegedly pushed Daniel came to me and apologized. "I'm really sorry," he said. "I didn't really hit him. I told him to move away from his brother. I'm still sorry, though, and I really didn't hit him."

I guess this boy thought I would be mad at him. I replied, "It's okay. Seth told me what happened and I am not at all mad. Thank you for sticking up for Seth and thank you for your apology. No one is in trouble."

I encouraged all three of them to move on and return to class. I thought little more of the scenario and was sitting there happily playing with my phone when the boy's dad came over.

"My boy doesn't put his hands on people," he said.

I felt he was being a bit defensive, and I hoped to end it before this turned into a thing. Trying to diffuse this nonissue situation, I said, "It's totally fine. The issue has been resolved."

Apparently, it was not fine. The dad added with assertiveness, "If my boy said he didn't hit your son, he didn't."

I nodded and fully agreed with him. I even added that I was sure he did not, but even if he had pushed Daniel, his son was in the right because he was defending my other son. "I've already talked to your son," I said, "and he was defending my younger son and it's okay. Daniel shouldn't have been messing with his brother."

Still, the dad was not satisfied. "Well," he continued, "my son apologized and he didn't hit anyone."

Trying to end this circular conversation, I decided to explain that my son was on the spectrum. "My son is autistic," I said, "and he thinks differently. Your son was standing up for my younger one, Seth. There is no issue here. Daniel is upset because your son stepped in and got in the way of him bothering Seth. Your son was not doing anything wrong, and I am not even slightly upset about this. It's *fine*."

However, I was thinking, *Go away now. Go away please? I want to watch shows on my phone in peace. C'mon, buddy, just let it go.* Instead of nodding and walking away, which was the desired outcome, the dad started asking questions. This was a risk. One of the results of sharing about my son's autism is having to educate and answer lots of questions. I got ready for a good long chat and gave up on my quiet hour of playing with my phone apps and watching my shows.

The father looked very surprised and said, "What do you mean autistic?"

How to answer such a broad question?

"Daniel is on the autism spectrum. He is autistic. He has a hard time seeing other people's perspective and is finding it difficult to accept that your son got involved."

The dad thought for a second and said, "Oh, you mean like that guy in the Tom Cruise movie, *Rain Man*? Well, he doesn't *look* autistic."

Rain Man is a movie that came out in the late 1980s that starred Tom Cruise and Dustin Hoffman. Dustin Hoffman played Raymond Babbitt, who was Tom Cruise's brother who is autistic with savant skills. Tom Cruise calls Raymond "Rain Man" as a nickname from when they were children. Kudos for this movie being made and starring a character who is autistic played by a famous movie star. I'm glad they put a character with autism so prominently on the big screen.

However, Raymond Babbitt is not the only person who is autistic.

Unfortunately, this father, and many others who are not as informed about the spectrum, think all people who are autistic or on the spectrum present themselves like Raymond Babbitt. Some people who are autistic are savants like Raymond Babbitt, and many are not. Some on the spectrum are nonverbal, some are highly verbal, some have savant-like skills, and others don't. Many fall somewhere in between. Daniel is autistic but he is not a savant. Daniel does not *look* like Rain Man at all and for many reasons.

I spent the rest of the class explaining how one person's autism could look totally different than another's, and that is exactly why it is called the autism *spectrum* disorder. This man got way more than he bargained for.

I left the martial arts studio irritated. I was mad that I had to explain my son, mad that I always had to explain his behavior, and mad that I was always getting him out of situations like this. I'm like Ray Donovan, the fixer.

What would have happened if I was not there? The dad would have had words with Daniel, Daniel would have had a temper tantrum, the dad would have been shocked, the instructors would have been called to the scene, then they would have called me, and I would have had to convince the instructors at the studio to not kick him out of the program. Maybe if people knew more about autism in general, I wouldn't have to educate this man who thought it's Rain Man or nothing. Everyone would know that not all people on the autism spectrum can count toothpicks by looking at a pile that falls on the floor. Nobody *looks* autistic either.

I am not alone in this. Many parents of children on the spectrum have commiserated with me about having their child being compared to Rain Man or having someone make a similar comment about their child "not looking autistic."

Sometimes I choose not to share Daniel's diagnosis just to avoid a lengthy conversation. Sometimes I will let people think we are just unkind humans to avoid a lengthy confrontation. A while ago, the whole family was on a shuttle from the parking lot at Baltimore Washington International to the airport. Daniel was sitting next to me when a stranger sat next to him. Daniel jumped up to move away from her and sit on my other side. The woman was clearly offended, and that's okay because it was a bit unexpected for him to get up as soon as she sat down. She proceeded to tell me she likes all of us equally, no matter what we look like.

"I'm okay if you're okay, but I think it's okay to sit next to everybody," she said.

I decided in this particular situation, I too was okay. It was a short shuttle ride. I made the call to not share our diagnosis with her. It wasn't worth it. I was more okay with her assuming my son was racist than understanding he was a child with autism who did not like to sit next to strangers. Daniel only liked to sit with family. Sometimes, the offended party just wants you to know they are offended.

In many scenarios I just haven't had the energy to engage. On a flight from Hawaii, Daniel got up to use the restroom. For some reason, Daniel likes to wait until the last minute before takeoff to use the restroom. This is just as the people are getting to their seats and moving toward the back of the plane, so Daniel has to push his way against the flow of traffic to get to the restroom. He's focused on the task at hand and not the fact that he is like a salmon swimming upstream. Often, I have to watch as people glare at him for going the wrong direction at a very inopportune time.

I, ever neurotic, never like to send Daniel alone anywhere, so I followed him. I watched Daniel bang on the door to the occupied bathroom. It was not a gentle or nice *tap, tap*. This was a full *bang, bang, bang* on the door. A message that clearly meant "Get out of the bathroom now!"

An elderly Asian woman came out furious. She said she was going to the bathroom when someone impatiently banged on the door. "How rude! Why all the banging?"

Daniel just moved right past her into the bathroom and closed the door, oblivious to this raging woman.

Since she looked like she wanted to blow off steam, I told her he was my son, and let her yell at me for a reasonable amount of time. I think I mumbled a few apologies and a "kids these days…" I could have explained he is autistic and has a hard time reading social cues, but I refrained. I felt like the situation had petered out, and I suspected there was a slight language barrier. I decided to just let it go.

Despite all the misinterpretation and negative interactions we have experienced together as a family, I feel like some really sweet things have happened to us as well. I'd like to give a shoutout to the Washington DC Metro conductors for their unbelievable kindness toward our family.

Daniel loved the Metro. He loved standing at the Metro station listening, watching, and even smelling the scents as the trains came in and out of the station. We would often visit the Metro station, and Daniel would stand there experiencing it for long periods of time. Daniel also liked to ride the Metro. From preschool through middle school, we would go on train riding outings we called "riding the rails." Daniel would go from one end of the red line to the other. He would run around in the car from one speaker to the next, listening to and recording the sounds of the trains.

One day, a conductor asked what Daniel was up to. Admittedly, he was behaving oddly, alternating between recording the sounds from the speakers and the tracks from the windows. We explained Daniel's interest in all things Metro and shared that he was especially interested in the different sounds of the trains. The conductor unexpectedly opened one of the partitions and gave Daniel full access to the window that allowed him to record whatever was holding his interest. This tiny act made our adventure an *experience*. What a kind person to notice that a child was so fascinated by something so random, didn't judge, and then even elevated the experience for him.

On a different Metro outing, Daniel and I were at the White Flint Metro Station. This was the year Metro introduced new trains into their fleet. It was anyone's guess which type of train was coming. Some days, Daniel wanted to ride the new trains. Other days, he wanted to ride the old trains. Also some days he would want to go one way in one type of train and return in the other. Due to Daniel's excellent hearing, he was able to hear the difference of the trains coming in.

I was usually prepped for these outings with an extra dose of patience. I knew I was in for the long haul. I knew I would be on the Metro for long periods of time and Daniel would have many specific requirements to be satisfied.

Sitting outside at the White Flint Metro, we waited for a new train to come in. We sat for quite a while waiting for the right train. At one point, a Metro employee came toward us with concern and curiosity. He was wondering why we weren't getting on any of the trains. Daniel and I explained we were waiting for a particular type of train to come in. Wouldn't you know it? The man got on his walkie and asked what kind of trains were due to come through to the station!

He even talked with Daniel for a while and was in awe of the fact that Daniel could tell by the different pitches what train was coming on which side. Another day made.

When we have these amazing and unexpected experiences, I make a point to share that Daniel is on the spectrum and that the special attention given to him makes a huge impact on our day.

Daniel loved the Metro so much it was the theme of his bar mitzvah. The invitation was a map of the Metro, the tables were Metro stations, and the décor was Metro themed. It was a hit.

On the eve of Daniel's bar mitzvah, we went to dinner at a restaurant. As we were waiting to be seated, Daniel saw a small boy with an iPhone. He got up real close to the boy to see the screen and said, "Oh! You're watching the Annoying Orange."

The mother was a bit unnerved by Daniel's proximity and said quite sternly, "Encroaching." That was her way of telling Daniel to move away from her son, but it went right over Daniel's head.

"Excuse me, you're encroaching," she said again, a bit more aggressively.

Knowing Daniel didn't understand, I jumped in and said apologetically, "Oh, I'm so sorry. I didn't notice my son was in your son's face."

I pulled Daniel away to give them space.

"My son wants to use the phone alone," the mother said. "He doesn't need your son to watch over his shoulder. He is too close."

I agreed with her and explained that Daniel was just excited to see someone else watching the Annoying Orange.

"Well," she said, "he's just too close to my son. Give him some space to play on his phone. He's encroaching."

I got the feeling she thought Daniel was behaving very oddly for a large thirteen-year-old and was very cautious. I just wanted to get us out of this situation.

I agreed with her and turned to Daniel. "Daniel," I said, "you need to give that boy space and let him play on his phone. Okay?"

I wanted to explain to her that my son wasn't being creepy, so I made the decision to tell her that Daniel is on the autism spectrum. I took a breath and said, "I'm sorry my son got in your son's space. He should not have done that. Daniel is on the autism spectrum, and he didn't understand you or the situation. I can see it unnerved you. I'm going to take him outside and explain that people need their space."

I walked Daniel outside and we talked it out. Yes, the boy had an iPhone. Yes, the boy was watching something Daniel knew and liked. But it was the boy's phone, and since we didn't know that boy, it's a social rule not to get too close. I told Daniel the mom didn't want him so close to her son because we are strangers to them.

Daniel was upset because he heard the mom use the "mean voice" when she had the aggressive and slightly angry tone. But I explained that she was in the right, and if a stranger got that close to Daniel, I'd be using my mean voice, too. I tried to explain this without making it seem like Daniel was in trouble because he was not. But he was not happy with the situation. We had been sitting outside for a while, so we went back inside. I figured the situation had blown over by then.

In this particular instance, sharing Daniel's diagnosis with the mother caused her to become defensive. I don't know how things get so twisted sometimes. When I came back inside with Daniel, a man approached and said, "Excuse me, can I talk to you a second?"

In my head I was shouting, *Yikes, now what? Who are you?* I put on my biggest smile and looked at him.

He said, "I'm that boy's father and there must have been some sort of misunderstanding. My wife didn't know your son is autistic and she doesn't have anything against autistic people."

I was slowly understanding the situation I had created. I smiled my best reassuring smile and said, "I didn't think she did. She would not have known he is autistic. I told her so she would understand why he was getting so close to her son. Daniel doesn't really get the concept of personal space. He is not able to really understand perspective taking."

The father seemed a bit guarded and said, "Well, good, because my wife didn't know."

I realized he thought that I thought she was a terrible person for being mad at my son. I explained further, "It's fine. I know she didn't know, and Daniel was the one in your son's space. I just took him outside to talk with him about it. Don't worry. I'm not at all upset and she shouldn't be upset either."

Once again, I smiled as big as I could and said I'd not taken offense. The father, seemingly placated and assured that I did not think ill of his wife, ended the conversation saying "Alright, respect." And I gave a peace sign.

At that exact moment, Greg came in from parking the car. He looked at me questioningly. I gave him a "I will explain it all later" look.

If the story had ended here, I could have written it off as an awesome learning and teaching experience for all involved. The couple for learning more about autism and Daniel for learning not to sneak up to watch other people's phones. But no. Daniel sporadically likes to take things to the next level. Sometimes he will do something so unanticipated he even shocks me. And I didn't think I could be shocked anymore.

As our table was ready, I ran over to the couple to say, "We are being seated. Hope you get seated soon and have a great dinner." More peace signs and respect. Closure. The couple did not respond with the smiles I had expected.

I turned around to find Daniel behind me pointing at them like he was going to "deal with them later" and mouthing "Youuuuu…" Aggressive move, Daniel. He was declaring war after I settled everything and had signed a mutual peace treaty. I rushed him away and had to apologize again.

Another favorite activity of Daniel's is bike riding. Daniel likes to ride his bike and recreate Disney or Hershey Park rides in his head as he goes around in circles or up and down hills. Daniel had been given permission years ago to ride up and down other people's hilly driveways. I had spoken to all of the parents and no one seemed to care.

One day, when Daniel was about fourteen, he came in from one of his bike rides. "Mama, you have to go yell at that man," he said.

I had so many questions. Another person may have led with an explanation and closed with, "And that's why you have to go talk to that man up the street." My child never gives me all of the information. He always gives me just enough information to confuse me, and then I have to play detective and solve the puzzle. We rarely have a dull moment in our lives.

"What man?" I asked. "Why? Who is he? What did he do? What happened? Did *you* do something?"

We know everyone on our block. As the only Asian person on the block and the nearby blocks, they all know me and my half-Asian boys. The house in question was a rental home. Families moved in and out, and I had not spoken to this family about Daniel riding his bike in their driveway because I had not realized the house had new renters.

Daniel had gone down this driveway on his bike, and the man had told him not to. Daniel had forgotten or ignored this instruction and apparently used it again. On this second offense, the man angrily told Daniel he was not to ride down his driveway because his small kids could get hurt. If Daniel did it again, he would call the police.

One of Daniel's triggers is being yelled at. He hates the mean voice. He even hates it when it's not directed at him. This is quite a problem as people use angry tones all over the place.

When this man yelled at Daniel and threatened him with the police, it was a double trigger. Daniel does not like the police. He thinks the police will take him away and I have no idea why. As it happened, this incident occurred early in the COVID-19 pandemic, so I could not just go knock on the guy's door to talk with him face to face about the incident.

After having the man pointed out to me a few times, I saw him taking out the trash. From a socially distanced space, I asked if I could talk with him. My intent was to apologize for Daniel forgetting he was not supposed to use his driveway and that if he had any more problems to please come find me and I would talk to Daniel. I was hoping he'd say "fine" and we'd wave goodbye courteously. This was not exactly how the encounter went down.

Somewhere between "I wanted to apologize for my son" and "have a nice day," he and I ended up in an argument. There was talk of how I should not teach my son it's okay to trespass on private property, how I need to check with everyone, and even a reprimand about how the old lady next door could get hurt. This was so out of the blue. I couldn't remember the last time I stood arguing with another grown adult in this manner. I tried to end the confrontation by asking him to not talk to my son again. I told him my son was on the spectrum and that he might misunderstand directions so please, in the future, bypass him and talk with me. He was shouting at my back as I was walking away saying something like, "What kind of a person threatens to call the police on a child?"

I came home to report to Daniel that I had "spoken" to the man up the street. I said the man had a very quick temper and he just yelled at Mom. Daniel was pretty shocked because it was hard for him to wrap his head around someone yelling at his mother. I warned Daniel that if he had any reason to talk with the man in the future, he should not. I told him to avoid the man all together.

"But what if he talks to me?" Daniel asked.

"Walk away and don't respond," I answered.

"But what if he yells at me?"

I suggested Daniel videotape the man on his phone and run to any other house on the block. I know all of our neighbors and they would call me. I'm a big fan of always having a plan.

"So, I can't talk to him?" Daniel asked.

"No, you cannot talk to him," I repeated. "He will start yelling just like he yelled at me and no one wants that."

To that, Daniel gave a sneaky little grin and said, "But I can give him the finger. Right? That's not talking."

I mean, what does a mom say to *that*?

Daniel has done this to me so many times. I feel like he is not understanding the situation at hand, yet he clearly does. Making aggressive gestures and suggesting he should give the man the finger leads me to believe he totally gets what's going on. This kind of dichotomy makes our autism so very hard to grasp.

It is much easier for me to think of one or the other—the limitations in comprehension or the uncanny ability to read the situation—yet these two skills are polar opposites. How is it possible to do both? On one hand, I am extremely grateful about Daniel's growth and ability to understand concepts because it proves he has the capacity. Then in the same moment, I get frustrated at why this skill can't be applied to all areas of life. It is so hard to acknowledge that his rate of growth and abilities range from area to area.

One night over dinner, Seth, who was just finishing middle school, and I were having a conversation. He was telling me about his trip to miniature golf with his friends. In the middle of recounting the good and bad shots and whose went in the water, Seth told me about an encounter, which he felt could have been racially driven.

Seth explained that as his friends—a mix of Asian, Black, and Latino boys—played, a Caucasian woman asked them to back up a bit. Since I was not there, I said it could have been racial or it could have been COVID-19 related and she wanted the boys to keep a safe social distance. Seth replayed the scenario in his mind. He concluded it could have been either, but he thought it was still a bit racial. I asked him how he reacted, and he said his friends all gave the woman space and moved on.

Daniel, who seldom pays attention to these conversations between Seth and me, jumped in with, "I would have yelled at her and told her I already have my freaking vaccine."

I had to take a moment to process this attack. I was shocked because really, in my opinion, his solution may have been one of the worst ideas for this kind of situation. Seth and I explained to him the merits of diffusing the situation and how charging at this woman and yelling at her would probably have ended in a multitude of negative outcomes. Daniel was unbothered. He was defending himself from her attack.

This is the exact reason why I can't sleep at night. I never know what Daniel will say or do. Imagine if this had actually played out? Imagine what would happen if the woman had a son or a husband with her who got in Daniel's face for yelling at her? What next? More words? Daniel would only react to the tone of voice and would most likely go on the attack. What if this got physical? There is no end to the spiraling.

That's when I decided it was time to get him a medical alert tag. I asked Daniel what he thought of it, explaining that if he ever got himself in a predicament, being able to show the other party he is on the spectrum may save him from the situation escalating out of control. He agreed.

I asked him if he wanted a necklace or a bracelet, and he chose a bracelet. Done. I ordered two online right then.

I was hoping it would work in similar fashion as the "student driver" stickers on cars. When I see those stickers, something in me softens. If a car with that bumper sticker on it acts erratically, I am more willing to give that person grace and forgive the turning-without-signaling move. Similarly, I hope that once a person knows my son is on the autism spectrum, whatever curious thing he is doing becomes significantly less offensive. I am hoping having a bracelet around his wrist will make it easier to let others know that Daniel is on the spectrum if words fail him or if I am not there to speak for him.

Over the years, I have gotten pretty good at knowing when to mention Daniel's autism and when not to. It's definitely a judgment call. If we are on a Metro train and Daniel starts recording all of the speakers, and people are giving him and me the stink eye, that is a time to say, "My son is on the autism spectrum and is fascinated by the audio of the train." This simple comment has had the ability to turn the stink eye into a very helpful or friendly person who is willing to discuss music and sound engineering with Daniel.

If we lived in a perfect world, people would not be giving dirty looks or making rude comments just loud enough for others to hear. We are not there yet as a society. This is why awareness is so important. Awareness and understanding can give us all a bit more patience.

CHAPTER 6

OPERATION GRANOLA BAR

I never thought food would be an issue area in our lives. Greg and I love food. In fact, we are fans of pretty much any cuisine. As a baby and a toddler, Daniel was a great eater. He ate all of the different flavors of baby food, all types of purees, and seemed to have no problems with sweet, savory, fruit, meat, anything. He loved playing with the food containers, too. I would clean out used containers and hand them to him to mess around with as I fed him his baby mush. He also liked to be fed outdoors. When my parents used to visit, they would put him in the highchair, the stroller, or even the swings at the park and feed him *al fresco*.

When Daniel began to self-feed and realized he could control what he was going to eat, the battles began. Daniel only liked to drink milk. Other children preferred juice and tolerated water but Daniel only wanted whole milk. I had to carry milk around with me, but milk is not easily portable on hot summer days. I purchased a small but sturdy cooler for this purpose. As all caregivers of young children know, we never travel lightly. The cooler was an additional item I had to remember to pack. I looked longingly at the other mothers who would whip out their water bottles, not having to worry about ice packs or insulated carriers. I hoped for the day I could just rely on a water fountain or even a juice box to pass to him from my purse.

By then, Daniel liked to eat very few things, so bringing snacks to playgrounds was not that simple. He did not want fruit or pretzels or the easy grab-and-go essentials like the other children. Daniel didn't even want the candy the other kids were crazy over. A friend of mine was shocked that Daniel didn't like chocolate M&Ms. We used to say that he just couldn't get past the candy coating.

Daniel liked bananas a lot. But I had to peel and slice it for him so it was a bit of a hassle to tote around a plastic knife and a paper plate. So what if I had to carry a tool kit and mini kitchen set with me everywhere I went? It's just part of being a mom.

After a while, we ended up with a very simple diet of baby oatmeal in the morning; bananas, blueberry Eggo waffles, and ham for lunch; and scrambled eggs at night. I was getting nervous about his nutrition due to the lack of variety of food groups and I brought it up with the doctor during a well visit. Our pediatrician suggested visiting a nutritionist. Before going to meet with her, the nutritionist asked me to keep a log of all the foods Daniel ate for about a week. That was easy, just write one day's worth and make seven copies.

I remember walking out of the nutritionist's office feeling like the worst mother ever. She told me that according to the list I provided, Daniel was deficient in every area—protein, vegetables, carbohydrates, and fruit. It felt like she was accusing me of depriving my child of the nutrition he needed out of spite. These thoughts were mere projections, but nonetheless I walked out significantly more down than when I walked in hoping for help and suggestions.

She suggested group classes for picky eaters where children play with food together or eat food as a group. Other food specialists suggested cooking classes for kids with their moms. Another therapist tried to give Daniel broccoli by building a forest with the stalks, playing with them like trees, and then trying it. This was unsuccessful. No way was that broccoli tree finding its way into the clenched jaws of my son.

One of the behavioral therapies I tried I called the "take a bite" method. It was very simple. Sit Daniel in the chair and tell him he could not leave until he took a bite of everything on the plate. The bites could be small bites, but he had to eat them.

Ah, the battle of wills began. The first day was a struggle to get Daniel in the chair. Thanks to safety belts on the highchairs, once he was in, he couldn't get out. Then it was a battle of wills to make him take a bite. And that's all you are allowed say: "Take a bite." No reactions, no emotions, no interest in what you are doing, just "take a bite" and reward with praise when he does. Daniel, in his whole two-year-old form, completely destroyed me. I started strong, but by the end of the first hour, I started a glass of wine. By the end of the second hour, I was done. And pretty drunk. Luckily for all of us, Greg came home from work and took over. He was probably very curious, but he saw me completely frustrated with Daniel just sitting there not eating. Greg picked up Daniel and got him ready for bed as I mumbled, "take a bite… take a bite… take a bite…" to myself.

It was not successful. Some could say it was an epic fail. I would agree. I visited a few more nutritionists and therapists for more advice. Most of them said similar things. "If the kid plays with the food, he will eat it," or, "If the child cooks the food, he will eat it." Yeah, no. As exciting as I made the meals look on the plate, my child was not interested. Someone said, "If you offer it on the table, eventually he will eat it." None of these approaches made a dent in Daniel's very limited diet.

After a while, we got into a groove. Other issues became more pressing so we would put the food issues on the back burner. Daniel got into a comfortable routine of the same breakfast, the same lunch, and the same dinner every single day. The good thing about his not liking many foods was that he never developed an interest in candy and junk food.

Between the ages of five and fourteen, Daniel started the day with Special K cereal. He ate about three bowls of it with whole milk every morning before school. When we traveled, he did not eat Special K because he would not drink milk outside the walls of our home for some reason. He also would not like just any kind of milk. It had to come from a glass jar. Otherwise, it "tastes different." I had registered with a milk delivery service for a while. They delivered whole milk weekly to our home straight from the farm. But that got tricky because some of the milk went bad in the summer heat. I once bought a cardboard carton of milk from Safeway. Daniel rejected the whole container. I resorted to saving the glass jars from the delivery service and buying gallon jugs at the Giant Supermarket as a backup plan. I would then pour the gallon into the glass jugs and put them in the fridge overnight. This seemed to be acceptable.

The trouble was when we were not home. Daniel would not pour milk onto a heaping bowl of Special K. He would leave it dry and then eat only a little, flake by flake. When my father saw this, he told me that Daniel was a "gentleman eater, very polite and tidy." For many years, we never ate out because Daniel would never consider eating anything a restaurant would have.

During elementary school, grilled cheese was added to our list of acceptable food items but only if we were eating out. If I made one at home, he would reject it. If I ordered it at a restaurant, he would eat it but only if the crust was removed.

Traveling was a bit difficult because I always worried about how and what to feed Daniel. This was a foreign concept for me. Growing up, my mom made dinner and we ate it. I had the benefit of having an excellent cook as a mother, but we still had meals I did not prefer. I never really had a choice in the matter and I never thought to question it or not eat it. Perhaps I was not head strong or creative enough to consider that as an option.

The next item Daniel seemed to eat in bulk was Barbara's Blueberry Burst Shredded Mini Cereal. I have no idea how this entered into our lives. I may have purchased it by mistake or in sheer desperation to find something to vary his diet. For some reason, he tolerated this brand of shredded cereal. I had to go to a separate supermarket for this one item, and I did so frequently without complaint because he ate it. This cereal also was very easily transportable, so I had baggies and containers filled with it in my car, my purse, and in my pantry. I'd leave a box of it at Daniel's camps or school so he would have something to snack on while the others enjoyed the group snack.

Then one day, as suddenly as he started eating it, he just stopped eating it. I asked Daniel what the story was and he said it tasted different. I couldn't taste a difference, but that was it. I opened box after box, asking him to try this batch or that batch. But this item had been burned from our list and kicked out of our lives. He had completely eliminated it from his diet. I still had a case of it in my pantry. To this day, Daniel will not touch Barbara's Blueberry Cereal.

Desperate to find another portable snack, I turned to what most children recognize in America: Goldfish crackers. Goldfish crackers are a staple in every child's life. Once again, I have no idea why Daniel finds Goldfish crackers acceptable. You would think my troubles were over because these are easy to travel with and carry around as a snack. Except not for us because we have Goldfish rules. First, Daniel will not eat just any kind of Goldfish. He only eats Baby Goldfish. I rue the day he was offered Baby Goldfish instead of plain Goldfish. Who did such a thing to him? To me! And he will only eat said Baby Goldfish if we are traveling in a car or possibly an airplane. This is not a snack I can pour into a bowl at home and say, "Have some Baby Goldfish so you don't get too hungry before dinner." Nope. We have to be in motion for him to enjoy this snack. I don't know why he says plain Goldfish taste different from Baby Goldfish because I think they taste exactly the same. I've often wanted to give Daniel a blind taste test of one of each and tell me if he knows which is which. He has not agreed to let me conduct this scientific experiment despite my multiple requests. Therefore, in my car I have Baby Goldfish in Ziploc bags for Daniel and plain Goldfish for Seth in case he wants a snack. Ridiculous, I know. But this is where I am. Don't judge. It's not nice.

Through the years, a few more food items were added and removed from the list in mini bursts. He would eat macaroni and cheese but only the kind that comes in cups. Definitely not the macaroni and cheese you make from a box. Now, neither is acceptable except if we are eating out and there is nothing else offered on the menu. Daniel will order macaroni and cheese off the kids' menu, but I first have to ask, "Are the noodles those skinny tube mushy things like in the Kraft box? And is the sauce real cheese or the powder the boxes use?" If the restaurant is fancy, they may have a gruyere mac and cheese or a delicious lobster mac and cheese. In these instances, or if the chef dares to use a penne or an elbow pasta, I know not to even bother with the order or I will end up eating it for him.

If only Daniel would eat plain rice, plain pasta, or even bread. French fries are another commonly found item. Every restaurant has one of these four items, and this would make life significantly easier for us. But none of these items make the cut. How can someone be half Japanese and not like rice?

Some days I don't think about it. Other days, I am reminded at meal times of the failure I am as a parent to have enabled my child to be so picky. Other times I just get mad about it. But no matter how mad I get, the problem never goes away and there is still a human to be fed, so I make the same meal over and over again.

A mom friend of mine once said that I was unbelievably lucky that I didn't even have to think about dinner for the kids because I just could make the same meals and have no need to meal plan. I guess it appears that way from her point of view. But it's a bit more complicated than just making the same meals over and over. The problem has developed many layers.

For example, Daniel likes to eat scrambled eggs for dinner every night. He likes to eat four eggs scrambled mixed with four-cheese Mexican shredded cheese. Every night at around six o'clock, I take out my frying pan, spray it with PAM, and make these eggs. Daniel likes to sit down and have a few bites of a granola cereal that has entered our lives in the past decade.

If I start cooking the eggs before he starts his snack, this is upsetting. He will not have enough time to snack on his granola during the time it takes me to scramble the eggs. I have to wait to get the "okay to turn on the burner" nod before I can start. Daniel wants his scrambled eggs to be "no wet, no dry, no brown, no different than the night before." He likes them piping hot off the pan and on the same plate every night.

Then, we have the geographical dilemma. Our house has three places to eat: in the middle of our kitchen at our island where three can sit comfortably; at our table in the nook attached to the kitchen, which seats four; and in the dining room that can seat more. We seldom eat in the dining room unless we have guests, so it is usually the two spaces in the kitchen. The kids and I eat at the island often when it's the three of us. If Greg is home, we like to sit at the table in the nook. Daniel does not eat eggs at the table. He only eats eggs at the island. Even if the rest of us are sitting at the table, Daniel will eat his eggs alone at the island.

For years we have been struggling with this. Sometimes I make him eggs first so Daniel can eat them at the island and then come join us at the table when he is done. Other times, he sits with us at the table, no plate in front of him and not eating, and I will make his eggs after we are done with our meal. Something changes in the flavor and the color of the eggs when he moves them from the island to the table apparently.

Daniel also never considers eating scrambled eggs outside of our house. Ever. Even if we are visiting my in-laws and I show him the same ingredients—the eggs, the spray and the cheese—he is not interested in eating the scrambled eggs. Hungry or not, rules are rules. Scrambled eggs are for home at the island and no wet, no brown, no different.

We did have surprising success with one challenge of finding something I can easily carry around that would curb his hunger when we were not home. I had been getting weary of carrying around a box of cereal, a plastic bowl, and a metal spoon as Daniel's portable snack. It had become enough of a nuisance that I decided to act on it. So I initiated the granola bar plan.

Daniel and I talked at length about how easy life would be if he could tolerate a power bar or granola bar that he could carry with him in case he got hungry. Being hungry and having low blood sugar is something every member in my family needs to avoid. And think of the convenience of pulling out a granola bar and snacking on it like other people! Not having to pull out a baggie with Special K pieces would be life changing. I was thinking ahead to possible future trips. We could go places with one less thing to stress about. I admit, having a handy, grab-and-go snack became a bit of an obsession for me.

The granola brand that Daniel likes to eat before I scramble his eggs is called Nature's Path Pumpkin Flax cereal. As luck would have it, Nature's Path makes a Pumpkin Flax granola bar. It is literally the cereal clusters in granola bar form. You would think I was the luckiest person on the planet! Except I was not. When making the cereal into a bar, the company added cinnamon. That was a big no. This granola bar was rejected. For the next month, I purchased and purged or forced myself to eat all the reject bars.

Then we finally found a bar he liked—a honey-flavored breakfast bar with protein. This was such a wonderful moment in my life! Over were the days of carrying my huge purse or backpack with cereal and bowls and spoons. Over were the days of wondering how to keep Daniel from becoming short tempered due to hunger. This was a success! Until it wasn't.

Somehow, when Daniel miraculously decided granola bars were going to be added into his diet, he stopped eating Special K completely. Daniel ate two protein breakfast bars in the morning and would not touch Special K with milk again. His dairy and fat intake was cut by one hundred percent. As an underweight growing boy, Daniel really needed the calories. And then, as if the gods were messing with me for messing with him, COVID-19 happened. Trips I had planned, one to Israel and one to Japan, were cancelled. To rub salt into my own wound, I had just purchased a case of Special K. Daniel would not touch any of that Special K. As pleased as I was that Daniel was able to add a new item to his list of edible foods, I was beyond frustrated at the elimination of the biggest meal of his day. I ended up giving that last case of Special K cereal to friends, making Krispy Treats, and using as breadcrumbs during the never-ending pandemic.

Every now and again, I get a crazy idea and try to hatch plans to see if I can expand Daniel's diet or see if he will eat something in a different location. I plot ways to desensitize Daniel, but I have not been able to unlock this mystery. Some parents say, "Your son will eat if he's hungry," or, "Don't make him a separate meal," or, "Just make him eat what you make for the family." I tried to see what would happen if I "waited until Daniel was hungry" when we went out of town for a weekend. Daniel gave Mahatma Gandhi a run for his money. Since Daniel could not find his usuals on our trip, he went from Friday night until we came home Sunday without eating. His complexion was gray and he ate about fifteen scrambled eggs that Sunday night. I fear what will happen if he suddenly stops eating eggs. The rigidity that inhibits him from changing his diet and the anxiety that fills him with fear of trying the unknown makes this food issue another enormous hurdle to overcome.

In the meantime, I have figured out ways to deal with the situation as it stands. Part of our home renovation was to build a pantry so I can stock foods Daniel eats in embarrassing quantities. If Daniel declares something his favorite, I buy it in bulk. If the cereal he tolerates now is the Pumpkin Flax Granola by Nature's Path, I buy huge bags of it from Costco. This cereal has granola chunks we call "clusters." Actually, we call the whole thing "clusters." Daniel never likes to share his food with me. I don't know if he thinks we will run out of his stash or if he doesn't want to share, but he does not like it when I eat his clusters. However, this is life, and I sometimes want a bowl of granola mixed with Cheerios. I have deduced that one of the reasons he does not like to share his clusters is because he specifically likes the big chunks of granola and he does not want me to eat them. So, when I eat a bowl of his cereal, I put the big chunks back in the cereal box. I do this even when he is not home. All to keep the peace.

Daniel also eats a specific kind of string cheese that is yellow and white made by Polly-O. At times, these are hard to come by. I usually check out three separate stores on three separate days of the week to see if I can be there when the dairy shelves are restocked. I have even made friends with the men in the dairy department at my local Giant. I have unloaded my dilemma to them that my son will only eat this specific brand of cheese stick, in this particular flavor, and I can never find it. They both know it shows up infrequently, so they keep a box in the back for me if it comes in, knowing I will be there on my weekly visits. If I am away and miss a week, they always ask if everything is okay at home because I didn't come in to check.

On the rare occasions that Daniel is with me when I run into the store for an item or two, I always check the dairy aisle. First, to see if the cheese sticks are on the shelves but also to have Daniel say hello to my friends and thank them for having his back.

When the topic of Daniel's picky eating would come up, I used to say flippantly, "It's fine. By Daniel's bar mitzvah he will be eating a bagel." His bar mitzvah came and went and no bagel was consumed. Another doctor told me not to worry, to view the changes in his diet in broad strokes. How is he doing at age five as compared to ten and fifteen? There has been no significant change to his diet since the boy grew teeth and started solid foods. Some days I feel defeated in this area or pretend it does not exist and live in my own bubble of denial. Other days, I am filled with hope because the granola bar plan worked.

CHAPTER 7

QUIRKS FOR GOOD NOT EVIL

Autism is a curious thing. It manifests itself in such different ways, and some can be so random it's hard to find people who can relate. Daniel has difficulty with social skills, but he does not have a hard time looking a person in the eye. Looking people directly in the eye is a common challenge for a lot of people on the autism spectrum, but not for Daniel. Each person on the autism spectrum has a unique set of issues. Daniel has a myriad of quirks that have presented themselves through the years. Some of these are amazing, some worrisome, and others are inexplicable.

One of the main concerns I have is Daniel's inability to read the room and react to subtle social cues. Interpreting facial expressions and understanding tone is also a tough skill to master. Sarcasm, jokes, and abstract meanings can be hard to discern when my son prefers concrete facts. Knowing what to say and how to say it is a very hard concept to teach. No matter how much practicing and role playing we do, I have no way to predict what will happen in every scenario.

Perspective is also hard because Daniel finds it very difficult to see things from a different point of view, especially in the moment. I often use puppets or drawings or stuffed animals to try and show various perspectives, but again this can only happen after the fact rather than in the moment.

On the positive side, I see a certain beauty in all of this. Daniel is not weighed down with the same insecurities as other children. He is not interested in what others are thinking. He doesn't really care about public opinion. To him, what he likes is what he likes. He does not try to conform or try to pretend he is something he is not. Daniel is his true self and does not know how to be anything else. I love this about him. I admire how he does not change himself for the comfort of others. I inadvertently changed something about myself when I first moved to America to fit in and assimilate. I often reflect upon this seemingly small change, and it still factors into my life daily.

My first name is Kuri. I am named after my mother's maiden name, Kurita, which is pronounced "koo-ri-ta" with the stress on the "koo" sound. My parents took the first part of that and named me Kuri, which is pronounced "koo-ri." In the winter of 1980, when I was a new kindergartener amongst all the Americans in my new environment, I had no idea there was such a thing as the "cooties." If you had the cooties, or touched someone with the cooties, this was a very bad thing. You would immediately have to go to a friend and get a cootie shot. "Circle circle, dot dot, now you have a cootie shot." If you say it out loud, "Koo-ri" sounds very similar to cootie. Kuri is not a common name in Japan and in my new American school, it was not just uncommon. It was unheard of.

When a friend of mine invited the class to a birthday party, she inadvertently changed the "u" in my name to an "o" and my name became a recognized and respectable American one—Kori. At the time, most people with that name were boys, but that was easier to accept for a group of young American children than the idea that I could be named after a fake germy disease like the cooties.

Suddenly, my friends were calling me Kori. At first, I didn't really know what was going on, and then it just took and became my name. I was Kori and the whole cooties thing was a thing of the past. I still go by Kori today because I find it easier to use than having to teach people how to say Kuri. When I meet someone, I introduce myself as Kori. I say, "My name is k-U-r-i, but it is pronounced Kori, like with an o." The new friend will naturally say Kori until they forget my name or look it up. Once the person sees my name in writing, they get confused. That "u" makes them second guess themselves and the pronunciation. Is it Kuri like curry? It can't possibly be Kori with a "u" in there.

With all of this confusion on a constant basis, I wonder why I never changed it back. I obviously had many opportunities to do so. When I started college, I could have insisted that I be called Kuri. People generally have grown out of the cooties game by college. I knew other people changing their names just for the sake of it and even changing their accents. I didn't do it.

My parents, my brother, and anyone I meet who is Japanese and speaks to me in Japanese refers to me as Kuri. I like having my family and Japanese community call me by the Japanese pronunciation because I don't want to erase it entirely. In the Japanese community, I'm asked if my name is Kaori, a different Japanese name, if they hear my American friends call me Kori because it sounds similar. I respond with, "No, my name is Kuri, you know, like the chestnut."

I think it was a way to separate my worlds—my English-speaking one and my Japanese-speaking one. It also was a glaring example of how I felt I had to change myself to fit in with both cultures. It is hard as a young, insecure girl to look entirely different from my mostly Caucasian friends and then have a foreign name that teachers stumbled over constantly. It was just easier to adopt an American first name and try to blend in at least with one part of my life. My last name gave people enough problems, but that was less of an oddity, as having a hard-to-pronounce last name is fairly common no matter what you look like.

Having a difficult name to pronounce has always made me feel singled out. It's the first thing I offer to identify myself and it's the first thing I see a reaction to. I had to change it (or it was changed for me) in elementary school to make finding friends easier. I remember wanting to be named Liz or Samantha.

I know what it feels like to not be accepted at face value and have to change to feel fully part of a group. I have lived it and I have experienced it thoroughly. I can deeply empathize and sympathize with my son when he feels like it is a struggle to jump into a conversation or join some kids sitting at a table. Greg and I chose American first names for both of our boys for this reason and at my request. We gave the children Japanese middle names so they could easily fit in and avoid being different. But seeing Daniel's resilience over the years, I don't think it would have mattered what we named him because he is strong and steady and true to himself.

Daniel has loved Disney from a very early age. He doesn't care if it's cool or not to others. It's what he likes. There was a phase when the movie *Frozen* became "so lame" among his friend group. Not to Daniel. He was steadfast in his adoration of Olaf and Anna. This makes me proud. He is also willing to speak his mind. He does not have the social filter that limits others from speaking their thoughts. Sometimes this gets us into awkward situations, like with Voldemort in the waiting room, but the intent is always pure and without malice.

As a toddler, Daniel once saw a very large man come to the house to repair the washer. He asked the man if he was a bear. The man explained he was a repair man but then took a moment to consider Daniel's comment and agreed that he was quite large, like a bear.

Once, when Daniel was in elementary school, we had to make a trip to the emergency room. Daniel saw some of the patients lying in cots and asked them if they were dying. "Are you dying? Mama, are they dying?" It was a legitimate question given the setting we were in. Was he concerned that the patients were now wondering if, in fact, they were dying? No, he was just curious and not stifled by social decorum. These moments give me a glimpse into his mind, and I admire how it is always thinking. Later, we had the conversation about "inside thoughts" versus "outside thoughts."

I think this inability to read the room and his unique ability to disregard public opinion gives him the courage to succeed on stage. He loves to perform in plays and musicals and does not seem to be hindered by stage fright or other concerns stemming from worrying about what others think of him. He is naturally musically gifted and that adds to his confidence in this arena. But even as a little child, if there was ever a request for a volunteer to get up on stage, Daniel would raise his hand. At a local school fair, Daniel thought nothing of jumping up at the age of five or six to sing a Beatles song during a karaoke contest in front of a blacktop full of people he didn't know.

When our neighbor invited us to go see her daughter perform at her middle school play, Daniel was so excited. The kids had been friends since preschool. The boys and I went together to cheer her on. She was great. At the curtain call, Daniel went to deliver flowers to her. Because the path was not clear to get to her in time, Daniel was a bit delayed and didn't quite make it when she got up to bow. Undeterred, Daniel walked straight up to the edge of the stage while others were bowing and called to our friend to step forward. She did and he handed her the bouquet. Seth couldn't believe it. He told me he would be too shy to do something like that. Daniel came back to his seat all smiles because he knew his flowers made his friend happy. Pure sweetness and oblivious to the looks our friend's daughter was getting as her classmates wondered who this boy was.

Daniel loves routines, schedules, order, and predictability. He does not particularly like it when life suddenly throws him a curve ball. An unannounced trip to the dentist may rock his world. Sometimes, this is frustrating and irritating, but other times I like to use this to my advantage. If a child thrives on routine, I will happily give him that.

Daniel has never had any problems with self-care because we set up a system. He has his particular soaps and shampoos that he likes to use, he has the way he likes to use them, and he has his daily routine. Once he gets out of the shower, he puts on his pajamas and goes to bed. When he takes off his clothes, he makes sure they are always right side out and brings them to the washing machine. These are just things he does. I never have to tell him or remind him. Once I learned to work within his routine, I have been able to avoid conflict.

For example, if Daniel showers in the afternoon because we went to the pool, his natural inclination would be to put on his pajamas and not leave the house for the rest of the day. Mostly, this is not a problem. However, if we happen to have plans to go to a friend's house after swimming, I will let him know ahead of time that he will not be able to get directly into his pajamas, and I'll confirm he is planning on putting on clothes afterward. If he accidentally puts on the pajamas, well, that's something I try to avoid. But still, working within the system has taught me to avoid some landmines.

Daniel also loves electronics. I think many kids do to some degree, but the love for electronics runs deep in Daniel. When we got our new washing machine, I told him it was electronic. It had a lot of cycles, a lot of buttons, a spinning dial, and lights that flashed. I showed him the settings I liked and how to use it. Bam! Another routine. And this one benefits me. Daniel can do laundry and can be counted on to put the washed clothes in the dryer. He never forgets to empty the lint tray or add a dryer sheet. It is fascinating how some things become set habits and other things do not, but I try to use his quirks for good.

Daniel also has an excellent memory. This can be troublesome when he never lets certain things go, but it is advantageous when he is able to learn all of the lines for his plays with ease. He even learns all of the other people's lines and has had to be reminded only to speak his own lines.

I lean on this strength often. If we are traveling and I need to remember the parking spot number in the garage, I just tell Daniel, "Hey, can you remember this for me?" And he will. I can ask him the name of the doctor we used to see when he broke his wrist, or what month he got his previous flu shot so I don't have to look it up. If Daniel remembers it, it is a fact. He remembers arbitrary things, too, like how the barber's floor looked different last time because it has since been retiled. He can remember the sound of the voice actor from animated movies and know what other characters he or she played in a different movie. Often, I marvel at how his brain works in such mysterious ways.

And then some quirks are just random. Daniel, at age two, liked pairing two items together with similar attributes. He would link disjoint (to us) objects in his mind and also physically in hand. Then they were cemented together as a "similar." These linked items have been the subject of many conversations, discussions, and the root of a significant number of issues. Some are funny now, but some are still ongoing and continue to mystify us.

The first similar was a plastic chicken wing and a plastic piece of steak that came from a pretend cooking set. We never understood the reason behind this pairing, but this was the very beginning of many sets of similars that are now a part of our lives. Daniel used to walk around the house with this fake chicken wing in one hand and a fake piece of steak in the other, saying, "Chicken, steak, chicken, steak…" as he went about his daily activities.

One of my favorite similars Daniel created was the colander and tiger set. I had a plastic step stool that was yellowish orange and had a tiger design. I also had a pink one like a pig and a white one like a cow. Somehow, Daniel linked the tiger step stool with a very large yellow plastic colander from the kitchen. One day the colander was in the cabinet, and the next it was a set with the tiger stool. From the inception of that similar, we had to travel with a strainer the size of a large watermelon and plastic step stool. This set I believe was due to the likeness of the color. Luckily, these items were light and easily transportable although very cumbersome.

Then there was the plastic ice cream and pickle; a tiny orange airplane and helicopter smaller than my palm; a sheep and pig; a Japanese superhero bath toy and a piece from the duck game; a bean from the Spill the Beans game and a bee from a Bee Hive game; and my ultimate nemesis, the tiny backpack that came off a mini-Diego figure and an orange cat the size of my thumb.

The similars were not limited to toys. Some were colors in the background of a TV show that flashed on the screen for seconds but matched a page in a picture book; a telescope from the opening scene of the *Toy Story* movie that looked a lot like the robot WALL-E from a different movie; the chords from one song that matched chords from a different song; and a character in a TV show and a character in a movie. Sometimes we obsessed over particular similar sets and sometimes they faded into oblivion. I never knew why some similars stuck around and some were passed on and forgotten. I stopped trying to figure out why the pairs were similar. Some were very obvious, but others were a mystery.

I would suggest similars to Daniel all the time. "Don't you think a donut is similar to a Cheerio? Can that be a similar?" I was trying to figure out the algorithm he was using. But Daniel has never inducted any of my pairs into his exclusive similars club because they do not work for him. I cannot seem to crack this code. I have found this fascinating and have taken it on as a challenge.

The reason I liked the tiger and colander pair was that they were big. I always knew where they were and we never lost sight of them. The smaller items were harder to track. Everything was all well and good when we knew where the similars were. But when they were missing, it was awful. Even worse was having just one half of a pair and the one reminded him that we had to find its other. We had to find both or there was a huge price to pay. Daniel was prone to major tantrums that lasted for very long periods of time. But finding a mini backpack from a mini-Diego was next to impossible. One time I had to stop a soccer practice and ask parents to look for a striped, gray mini cat from a play mobile set because Daniel dropped it in the field. I organized the parents in a grid-like pattern. We found it. The day was saved. This is how far I would go to avoid Daniel's major tantrums.

Daniel had a toy tractor truck that sang the "Old McDonald" song, but it stopped playing the music so I got rid of it. I didn't get rid of the animals that rode the tractor because the pig and sheep were his favorites. They were a hardcore similar. He liked to hold one in each hand and shake them back and forth. I think this was somehow self-soothing. These creatures were small but not tiny. They fit in my palm. Daniel would take these everywhere—*shake, shake, shake*—put them down and forget. Only if I was very vigilant would they make it home. Until one day they didn't.

Daniel had such a fit and talked and talked and talked about his beloved pig and sheep so much I started the futile quest for a new tractor set. For a child with language delays, Daniel could talk endlessly about a certain topic if he wanted it badly enough. I looked online. I looked at Toys "R" Us. I looked on eBay. I looked at every Target in my driving distance. I had given up hope because this was an old toy. Daniel had gotten it when he was in preschool, and at this point he was in grade school. As a last-ditch effort, I wrote to the toy company. (Pro tip: A lot of toy companies will replace parts for the price of shipping.) I asked if the tractor was still available to buy. It turns out the toy was no longer being manufactured.

Just when I had given up hope, I got an email from someone in the company. He asked if I was talking about a tractor with a farmer and some plastic animals. I had that feeling of almost winning a huge prize but not wanting to get ahead of myself. The man had kept the animals from that same toy and they were sitting on a shelf in his office. But he wasn't sure he kept the whole set. I asked about the pink pig and white sheep. He responded he did have those two! And he offered to send them to me. I was so happy I cried. These are the things that made me believe in the goodness of humans. I look back now and think, *Wow, how in the world did that happen?* But it did. When I gave these to Daniel, he was so happy he immediately took one in each hand and shook them gleefully. They are still on display on a bookshelf in his room.

When we visited my parents on vacation, I would warn my mom that Daniel would probably create some similars and things would get moved around. My mom, who was ridiculously strict with me and my brother, was the complete opposite when it came to my children. I was in shock when I first witnessed my mom letting my kids get away with anything and everything. Climbing on the coffee table? No problem. Eating on the floor? Sure.

One morning, my parents overslept. Their alarm clock had disappeared. My parents' alarm clock was circular and similar to the cooking timer in shape. Daniel had found a new set of similars. He walked around with these two items, one in each hand with his patented *shake, shake, shake*. Once we figured out where Daniel had put them, my parents had to sleep with the clock and the timer next to each other until morning when Daniel would once again walk around with them. During a quick two-week visit, this behavior was cute.

My parents were totally fine with it and conformed to the rules of the similars with ease.

One day, I asked Daniel what my similar was. He told me with a straight face that it was the witch from *The Wizard of Oz*. "The one with the green face, Mama." He was probably five at the time, but still, ouch. Apparently, this is no longer the case. It's unclear when I ceased to be similar with the witch. But just knowing I was associated with someone so ugly, mean, and green, well c'mon, it hurt my feelings. How could it not? Autism, I blame you.

I have learned that Daniel likes things a certain way. In a way, I guess we all do. I have a favorite pillow. I have a favorite seat at the kitchen island. I could do without these things but why should I? I have learned to appreciate Daniel's preferences too. I know which shirts are Daniel's favorites, which towels he prefers, and which shoes he likes to wear. This can have benefits now that he is older. When sending Daniel to summer camp, I never have to worry about Daniel leaving his towels behind at the pool or his lunch box at the tables. I know with certainty that Daniel will come home with the exact items I sent with him.

Seth, who is the complete opposite of Daniel, never formed attachments to things. Seth would go to the same camp with the same items as his brother but come home with only half of his possessions. Seth didn't need to have that exact item the next day, so he was less careful with his belongings. One day, Seth came home with one shoe missing. I have no idea how that's even possible but he did.

I can't fully resent all of Daniel's quirks because some of them are his superpowers.

CHAPTER 8

FIND A HOBBY, GET A DOG

―

Parenting our boys has been a unique experience filled with new adventures daily. I don't think anyone gets practice at parenting beforehand. We are all thrown into the deep end starting at day one.

When it was my turn to parent, I was very conflicted with how to raise my American kids. I knew I wanted to be involved in my children's education. Due to the language barrier, my parents were not able to help me with my homework as much as I had hoped. My parents also were not comfortable attending events that required them to interact in English. Because of the cultural differences, my parents had to learn how to throw birthday parties at the house with clowns and cake or at the roller-skating rink with the back room for pizza. They did not know about celebrations like sweet sixteens, proms, or after prom.

I had the benefit of being able to speak English and being immersed in the culture. I knew from day one I wanted to be a very present and involved parent. One thing I made a priority was attending all of my children's events. If there was a school party or a concert, if my boys were on stage, I was always in the audience. I also tried to get to know the parents of a lot of the boys' friends. I never wanted my child without a parent on Parents' Day, and I often volunteered to be a temporary parent to the children who did not have one present. This was very important to me.

I also had a learning curve to how I was going to parent. Would I be strict? Would I be lenient? I tried to be effusive with praise but this did not feel natural. I also was brutally honest, but this did not feel kind. When the kids started piano lessons, I told them truthfully if I thought they played poorly. But I showed them how to improve or where their mistakes were. When they fixed it or played better, I noticed and gave the appropriate praise. When Seth started singing and he sounded nasally, I told him he could improve by singing more from his stomach. A friend of mine overheard and was shocked that I was being so honest. In my culture, at least between family, if you were bad at something they told you. If you said or did something stupid, someone informed you of the error. I did not grow up thinking this was mean or insulting. I just thought it was natural. In America, however, people are kinder with their words and gentler with their delivery.

One year, Seth had a recital at his elementary school. Seth was in first or second grade and he was going to play a piece on the piano. Greg, Daniel, and I were sitting in the audience anticipating his performance. Seth dutifully got up on stage, took his bow, sat up at the piano, and played his song. He completed the performance with gusto, stood up, took his closing bow, and proudly walked off the stage with his head held high. I clapped and cheered and yelled, "Go, Seth! Great job!"

And then Daniel and I looked at each other. "Did he just play only half of the piece?"

I know Greg did not notice this omission of the second half of the song, but I sat there completely perplexed. What should I do in this situation? The American mom in me wanted to say "Great job! You played well. You didn't make any mistakes and you walked off confidently. Great bow!" Did I even mention the hiccup?

But the Japanese mom in me wanted to say, "What in the world was that? You only played half the song. I'm glad you were able to pull it off because your finish was strong, but what *was* that?"

Daniel was asking me the same questions. "Mama, why didn't he play the whole thing? Did he mess up? Did he do it on purpose?"

All great questions, I thought. I sat wondering what I was going to do, what I should do, and eventually what I would end up doing. I knew if I spoke to him the way my mom would have, Seth would have been very upset. I decided I would do a mixture. I ended up telling him he did a great job, because he did, but then I brought up the fact that he neglected to finish his piece.

Seth admitted that he got a bit of stage fright and decided to stop early. I was still confused, but I told him that although that was a strange thing to do, he finished with a flourish and no one, not even Dad, knew what had happened. I told him he obviously couldn't get it past Daniel, but other than that, no one else seemed to be the wiser.

I was told by my therapist that I did the right thing. I was right not to attack Seth but to acknowledge the areas where he did well. And I was not wrong to ask why he did what he did. The most important part was that Seth felt supported.

I called my mom up later that night and relayed the story. Just like I knew she would, she said, "Stage fright? What is he, seven? He should have just played the whole song."

This comment comforted me because it made me feel validated for reacting the way I did. I felt like I was being too soft on my son. But knowing he felt reassured by what I actually said was validation as well.

Parenting is hard. There are so many tips and books and therapists and therapies. But as many strategies as there are, there are even more different kinds of children. Even between siblings, it is hard to parent them exactly the same. I have come to realize that the parenting part will always be hard. There are different stages and none of them is easy.

Without knowing it, I compiled a bit of a survival kit to make days easier for me. So much advice exists for self-care—have a hobby, go to therapy, eat healthy, meditate, exercise, or even get a dog. Some work and some do not. But like all things, I gave everything a try and also came up with a few tricks.

One thing I have found to be extremely helpful is to have at least three neutral topics to converse about as a survival mechanism. This is useful in pretty much any social situation, but as a mother of a special needs child, many times I am stuck in a conversation that I would like to escape. I use these topics when I am in a situation where, for example, a mom is bragging about her child and I am not in the space to listen to someone else's successes. It also comes in handy when I am with a Negative Nancy who likes to complain about life. My three topics are usually any weather topic, a great recipe, or a great book I am reading. Having my conversations ready makes me prepared to face the world on days I am not up to it.

Knowing how to look busy and having ways to kill time are also important skills to master. Many therapy sessions, doctor visits, and various appointments are a part of being a parent. In the age of on-demand shows on my phone, I always have a few episodes of a series downloaded. You never know how strong the Wi-Fi will be. These are perfect because each episode usually lasts around forty minutes, which is about the time of the appointment.

I have become addicted to all sorts of crime dramas. Greg would ask what I'm up to and I'd tell him, "Oh, I have a whole bunch of case files to get through," referring to my crime shows. I enjoy these shows partly because of the escape from my reality and the idea that "at least I'm not facing a prison sentence for burning down the wrong person's house. My life could be so much worse." I enjoy the fact that at the end of each episode, there is a resolution. The bad guy is caught. I crave that closure. As my life and the lives of our children are so unpredictable and uncertain, I need to feel that happy ending. Case closed. At least it's there in my fictional escapes.

A lot of driving is also involved as my children go to different schools or attend different classes and activities. For these long periods of time, I listen to podcasts. I have a few podcasts queued in my virtual library. These are perfect to cure my boredom and helpful if I am having a bad day and need to distract myself from my anxious thoughts.

There is no end to the amount of information available in audio form these days. The free library app has unlimited audio books available and is also a great way to entertain myself as I drive around in my car. One year Seth was in a private school in DC, Daniel was in a private school in Maryland, and neither had a bus service. I would spend an average of four hours in the car on a school day. I listened to a lot of books during this time. I try not to listen only to fiction, which is my preference. I will usually listen to what

I call a learning book every third or fourth book. I feel like less of a slacker if I actually learn something every once in a while. The books can be about anything—habit forming, organization, autism. These books help me feel somewhat productive and give me fodder for my neutral topics to keep at hand.

Having the boys at two different schools stretched the limits of my brain. It was hard to keep all of the pajama days, half days, no school days, teacher workdays, test days, and wear red days straight. My solution was to color code them. Each child had a color. Seth was green and Daniel was blue. From jackets to cups to towels, each one had his respective color. Naturally, I color coded their paperwork. Daniel had blue folders for his records and Seth had green. I also created color coded binders. This seems like an extreme solution, but I feel it's worthy of a mention as it has helped me tremendously.

The binder turned out to be very handy for all of Daniel's Individual Education Plan (IEP) meetings. Having the documents in one place made attending the meetings less stressful. Knowing where all the necessary paperwork was located was also helpful in preparing for the meetings. Walking into the conference room with all of the members of the IEP team with a binder in hand gave the illusion that I was very organized and ready to go. Whether I was or not, when I opened my binder and pulled out the most recent IEP draft, someone would compliment me on being an involved parent. A binder, it's that simple. This would set a positive tone right away, which, in my opinion, is quite beneficial to having a productive meeting.

Music and snacks are also imperative in my survival kit. I have a go-to playlist and theme song for when I need a pick-me-up. "Mambo No. 5" by Lou Bega can put me in a good mood just by humming it. I always have Cheetos and Twix bars handy, a mix of savory and sweet for when I know I want to sit and sulk for a bit and stare aimlessly at a wall.

Stocking my car with snacks for me and the kids has been helpful. My kids hate traveling in Dad's car because it does not have the snacks, water, and other lifesaving supplies that Mom's car has. My car has pillows. When you spend as much time in the car as I do, it is important to bring some pillows along. Why be uncomfortable during those long stretches of waiting? My sons' friends also like my car because there is always a selection of goodies.

Other things I like to keep on hand are a few thousand-piece puzzles. I started buying puzzles because I thought the kids would like it. There is no winning or losing and there are no tricky instructions. I had not anticipated the complete lack of interest from both my children. But I was hooked. I like the feeling of spreading out the pieces, separating them by color or patterns, and then putting them together. Organizing and sorting all the bits into a final product that makes sense of the chaos is cathartic. It's another bit of closure and control. The physical sense of taking nonsense and making it into a complete image makes me feel content.

I tried other activities like knitting, crossword puzzles, and adult coloring books. But I did not like them as much. Knowing I have some tricks ready to decompress has made me feel more prepared and able to handle some of the crazy days of chaos.

The biggest suggestion I finally agreed to was the dog. Getting a dog kept coming up, and I resisted with a vengeance. Despite the recommendations from practically every specialist we saw, and the clear visual proof that every time

Daniel was with a dog he settled down and his anxiety dissipated, I flatly refused to get one. Greg grew up with a dog, and he was all for it. I have major allergies so I was against it. I also never had a dog, so the whole experience was foreign to me. In this one area, Greg and I could not agree. I did not want to have to walk a dog, feed a dog, worry about a dog, or everything and anything I had heard of with regard to dog ownership. This sounded like the exact opposite of a way for me to cope. I wanted nothing to do with it.

We couldn't even agree on the hypothetical dog we would never get. I wanted a small, hypoallergenic dog that could fit in a purse. Greg wanted a dog large enough not to be mistaken for a rodent. Daniel wanted a "dog that always stays a puppy" like a Maltese. So because we could not agree on a breed, and because of my allergies, it was easy for me to keep the family at bay and deny them a canine comfort animal.

I held out for about a decade. But when Daniel turned thirteen and Seth turned eleven, they broke me down. That summer, I caved and our family got a dog. The breeder was highly recommended by our neighbors and they were even willing to drive the puppy to our house from four hours away. They could not have made the transaction any easier. We made the commitment.

The arrival imminent, we bought the crate, food bowls, chew toys, and the boys picked out a name. Then Lucky entered our lives.

This was an interesting transition. Daniel was in love. I had heard having a dog could help with social skills and language development, and I was fascinated to see it in action. While all of us were talking to the puppy like a baby, with high-pitched voices and "coo, coo," sounds, Daniel was different. He'd say, "You can lick me now." Or, "Hello, Lucky. You can bark now."

And, "Lucky, I am going to pet you now." It was as if Daniel was speaking to a person, not a new baby fluffy puppy.

This was surprising because everyone else instinctively talked to the puppy in a higher-pitched, sugar-sweet tone. Only Daniel spoke to Lucky like a regular person. What was interesting was Daniel did not notice he was doing anything differently than the rest of us. Despite the odd manner of speech, the two of them completely bonded. You can often find them sitting together, wordlessly, Lucky curled in a ball at Daniel's feet. It may be the sweetest thing to see.

The interaction with the two developed as well. Training Lucky was very educational for me. We used a click-treat method to teach him tricks. Sit, down, touch, drop it, and such. Because this method is behavior based, the person who picked it up the fastest was Daniel. It was amazing. The trainer was impressed Daniel knew exactly when to click and reward the dog. That's when I realized of course Daniel would be great at training because this is how he learned with verbal behavior. That, too, was a behavior-based method. It was fascinating to see it come back full circle.

We were all learning how to deal with Lucky. I had never had a dog before and knew nothing about crate training or house training a dog. Even walking the dog was a new experience. I did not know dogs don't naturally take to a leash and go for long walks. At first, Lucky barely left the front yard. Then he would go a few feet and lie flat on the ground, refusing to move another step. Sometimes we would have to pick him up and carry him far away enough from home that he would want to walk back. All of these events would get very frustrating because Lucky just wasn't listening. Sometimes I would catch us yelling at Lucky and getting angry with him. These turned out to be great teaching moments and I tried to use these as perspective-taking opportunities. Why are we yelling at the dog? Because we are frustrated. Why are we frustrated? Because he doesn't listen. Why does Mom yell at you? Because I sometimes don't listen.

When Lucky was training, we would reward with treats. Once Lucky would learn a new command we would wean the treats. I tried to use this as another teaching opportunity. Lucky performs the trick because he knows he will get a treat. He knows if he behaves in a certain way, he will be rewarded with a good snack. I tried to make a parallel and said that if Daniel was nice to Seth (didn't copy him, or didn't aggravate him), Seth would be nice to Daniel in return. I encouraged Daniel to be flexible and nice to his brother by letting Seth choose the activities or show or videogame sometimes. Seth might then want to hang out with Daniel more and more. We are always working on this, but having Lucky to use as an example has helped in explaining and describing social stories.

I started to see that getting Lucky was the best thing we did for our family. He gives Daniel someone to play with instead of trying to take out his boredom on his brother. Lucky provides unlimited emotional support and calms both kids if they are feeling anxious. Just holding the guy is enough to put us all into a Zen place. The breeder estimated that our dog would be a small eighteen-pound Mini Cockapoo. He ended up growing to be about thirty pounds, so Greg is also pleased as punch.

Just as the therapists recommended, Lucky became a comfort for me, too. Something about having a dog around is calming. He makes us laugh, he gets us outside, he helps me teach the kids about responsibility, and he's just a fun guy. Using Lucky as a teaching tool makes things more concrete for Daniel. Adding him into my survival kit has been one of the best learning experiences I have had to date.

These are just some of the things I have tried in order to maintain my sanity. Like I said, parenting is hard, and it does not look like it will stop being hard. Stashing candy bars and getting lost in a murder mystery are my ways of dealing with the days that don't go exactly the way I expected.

I tell my kids that every day is a new day. Every day is a chance to start fresh. Daniel takes this to heart. When we have a terrible day of fighting, yelling, and hurt feelings, I try my best to handle the situation at hand. I try really hard to stay calm and explain why I am upset. Sometimes I just tell Daniel that I am not able to have a conversation and need my own time-out to calm myself before we can start the process of making up. It's hard not to hold a grudge and it's hard to let things go. I have the kind of personality that likes to keep score. But inevitably, the next day arrives and I am greeted by a shy Daniel who asks me, "Mama, is today a new day?"

I try to respond with positivity and say, "Yup! Today is a new day. Let's start fresh."

If I say it cheerfully, I start to kind of feel cheerful and hopeful that today actually is a new day.

CHAPTER 9

EVEN DAYS AND ODD DAYS

The Maddux School ended in second grade, and I had to start a new school search for Daniel. Once again, I went on tour after tour of private schools in the area. I decided not to place Daniel in our public school because the school was still being renovated and the classroom sizes were double what he was used to at Maddux.

As part of the process of applying and finding a new school for Daniel, he had to get tested by a neuropsychologist. Daniel was tested for two days. About a month later, we were given the results by the doctors. This was when we were officially told Daniel was on the autism spectrum and no longer PDD-NOS. This news did not come as a shock to any of us. We knew of the challenges both socially and academically and we knew nothing in our lives would change whether we called it PDD-NOS or autism.

After accepting Daniel's autism diagnosis, the next step was determining how to share this with both kids. Greg and I tossed and turned about this conversation. When do we tell

Daniel about his diagnosis? Will he know what this means? Will Daniel be upset? How will he react? How do we explain this to him so he doesn't think different is bad? Greg and I talked about it, delayed the conversation, talked about it some more, and delayed the conversation some more. Finally, when Daniel was about ten years old, and Seth was eight, we broke the news to both kids separately.

When we told Seth that Daniel was on the autism spectrum, he looked at us like he already knew. "Ah, no kidding."

Even two years younger than Daniel, Seth was able to deduce Daniel was different, and now he had a name for it. He took the news in stride and the world kept turning. That was painless and easy, so onward we pressed and went into Daniel's room.

A book was recommended to us titled *All Cats Have Asperger Syndrome* by Kathy Hoopmann to help initiate the conversation. Although Daniel does not have Asperger Syndrome, we used it as a starting point. Asperger Syndrome is no longer a medical diagnosis. It is now considered part of the autism spectrum. The book shows pictures of cats doing things differently and is a nice tool for discussing being different and being on the spectrum. After we read the book with him, we talked about the title, the diagnosis, the special things that make Daniel unique.

Daniel's reaction was, "How did they get all these cats to pose like this in the book?"

He was fully aware he had quirks that made him different, and really all he wanted to know was about the cats.

This conversation captures so much of my parenting experiences with Daniel. I worry. I fret. I overthink. In the end, the best solution has always been to just plow right through it. For Daniel, knowing he is on the spectrum has helped him. He is able to recognize some of the things he does may not be mainstream, and now he has a name to associate with why he behaves this way.

At the start of third grade, Daniel was at a new school in the area that specialized in high-functioning children on the spectrum. Where Maddux had children with a wide range of mild issues, the students at the Auburn School were very similar in profile to Daniel. It seemed to be a good fit. After visiting it, Daniel said, "Mama, I think I will go here next year."

Daniel had been on a handful of school visits with us, but this was the only time he said something like that. Daniel had told me he didn't know other children out there were also autistic. But when he started at this new school, some of the other students shared their own diagnosis.

This was an interesting time for us as a family. Daniel was now surrounded with friends who understood each other. Some children wore noise-cancelling headphones, and Daniel could relate as we used to carry around ear plugs to turn down the volume for him in crowded places or movie theaters. Having students around who proudly shared their autism was one of the reasons this environment was a success. This new school was a very safe space for Daniel. He was never singled out for being different, nor did he feel isolated by his peers. They were all connected by their shared experiences of being similarly unique.

After we told Daniel about his diagnosis, it became much easier for us to talk to him about his quirks and vice versa. For example, Daniel likes to listen to multiple versions of one song. If a song is recorded by the original artist and then remade, he likes to listen to them back to back. This can be irritating to some, but he loves it.

When he would play me a song and it moved to the next version, I'd say, "Oh, I just wanted to hear it once. I was going to go do something." Daniel would answer, "Sorry, Mom, it's because I'm autistic. I just like it this way."

It has given him the tool he needs to sort out some of the interesting idiosyncrasies of his personality. The middle school years were filled with many things he liked to do because "I just like it this way."

A large way in which autism manifested itself in Daniel was through rigidity. His inflexibility makes things very difficult for all involved. One of Daniel's therapists used spaghetti as a visual. If you try to bend an uncooked spaghetti stick, it breaks. But if it is boiled and flexible, it will bend. Asking a rigid child to not be rigid is challenging.

Some parents say, "Oh, my child is stubborn or hard-headed." But the level of rigidity in Daniel exceeds the kind of stubbornness people typically envision. Some children can be bribed or reasoned with, and some kids even will change their course for fear of punishment. Our rigidity is a mountain that cannot be moved.

One thing that must always be a certain way is the remote control. It was once convenient to have Daniel turn on the TV because I did not know how. But this convenience turned into a major trigger and continues still. Because we let Daniel be the person who turns on the TV, he became stuck on the idea that he is the only person allowed to do so. Only Daniel turns the TV on or off, selects the show from the menu, and fast forwards or rewinds. Daniel controls the remote all of the time, whether he is watching alone, or we are watching as a family.

If we are watching our favorite family TV show, *America's Funniest Videos*, Daniel has to grab the remote, turn the TV on, and be the one who skips the commercials. If he has to leave in the middle of the show to get a glass of water or a snack, he takes the remote with him while we just sit and wait. This can get a bit tedious. After the show ends, if Greg wants to watch football or basketball, Daniel will switch on the sports, even though he is leaving the room. Only when it is clear that Daniel is ready to give up the remote is Greg allowed to have it.

This has ruined many family nights. Sometimes it's just faster for Greg to search through the screens but that ends up in a tumultuous tantrum, which then leads to one of us walking off in a huff, thus abruptly ending family night. What is the solution to this? Do we just let him do what he does so we can at least enjoy an evening together? Do we work on rigidity and power through the tantrums to make a point? A therapist told me that if I dig my heels in, I am modeling rigid behavior to try and end Daniel's rigid behavior. But to that point, if I don't dig my heels in, am I just letting Daniel do whatever he wants? I often wonder if I am doing any of this "right."

Being rigid or getting stuck is the cause of almost all the fighting that happens in our home. For example, Daniel was stuck on always being the first to do something. Daniel and Seth share a bathroom that is between their bedrooms. In the mornings, Daniel would hide the toothpaste from Seth so he could brush his teeth first. This led to many mornings starting off on the wrong foot until we moved Seth out of that bathroom and into the guest bathroom. These rigidity issues just pop up. One day, there was no toothpaste problem. Then suddenly, it was a major issue.

Daniel and Seth have taken piano lessons from a very early age and practiced every day. Then Daniel needed to practice the piano first. He started practicing the piano before school, but these sessions were so rushed that I said he had to practice when he had more time. When the kids got home from school, Daniel would forget about the piano until Seth decided to practice. Then Daniel would get mad at Seth for not letting him go first.

These arguments became so tedious that I assigned the boys even days and odd days. On even days, Daniel practiced first and on odd days, Seth did. This was a great solution except the few times in the year when two odd days happened in a row at the end of the month. Then Seth practiced first two days in a row and that was just not acceptable.

I never know when the other shoe will drop because I never know what the next issue will be. Daniel has to go first, he has to eat at a certain seat at the island, he has to be the one who manages the music during meals, he has to be the one who turns on the Xbox, the list goes on and on and on. There usually is no *why* involved.

I'd say, "Daniel, please let Seth turn on the TV."

He'd reply, "No, I have to do it."

I'd answer, "If Seth always turned on the TV every time, that would be unfair and you would be upset. Can you please just hand him the remote?"

Daniel would respond, "No, only I can do it. Not Seth because it's my rule."

Rigidity or inflexibility is one of our biggest challenges and has been very difficult to reconcile. Daniel's rigidity keeps him from being able to see other people's perspectives. He can only see his own side. It can be positive in that he is not really prone to peer pressure, but it can also be a major negative.

This extreme rigidity makes Daniel present as selfish and self-centered. It's his way or the highway. But he is not selfish.

He is actually a super sweet kid who can't see how his actions and words are affecting others. He is the child who will yell in a packed movie theater, "Mama, this is your favorite song! Aren't you so happy?" because knowing I am enjoying the song "Hello" by Lionel Richie during the *Paddington Bear* movie just elevated this movie for him a thousandfold. His life goal is not to frustrate those around him with his inability to be flexible. Rigidity is a beast, and it has a very strong hold on him.

Part of what makes it so hard is the randomness of his rigidity. I have learned to stop asking why he is stuck on certain things, like choosing music or having to be first, because I may never understand. What I struggle with is trying to explain how these rigid thoughts are keeping him from attempting different things. It pains me to see the opportunities he is keeping himself from out of fear of stepping out of his comfort zone. If you always have to go first, or if you always have to win, you can't participate in any activities in which you may not go first or you may not win. I have seen him tell teachers and counselors that he does not want to participate in a particular game because it is a "winning or losing game." I truly envy families who have game nights. There are not many games we can play that don't involve winning or losing.

Music is a major part of our family. Daniel and Seth are both naturally musical. We often sing songs together in three-part harmony. I grew up playing the piano since I was three years old. Greg is an incredible guitarist and can play classical, jazz, and rock. Greg and I introduced our children to all types of music from an early age. We played the obligatory children's music CDs from Raffi to Laurie Berkner, but we also included the likes of Bob Marley, the Beatles, Queen, and more.

Greg and I are big fans of classic rock. It's the one genre we agree on. But we no longer rock out to music when we eat dinner or hang out in the kitchen. We can't. If I slip up and let it happen by mistake, inevitably an argument follows.

Seth will say, "Let's listen to Post Malone."

And Daniel will say, "No, we are listening to Paul Simon."

Then I jump in with, "We can all take turns."

This turns into "No! No!" And bam! A meal ruined.

This saddens me on many levels. One, I no longer can enjoy music in my kitchen for fear of an incident. But two, if you are the only person allowed to manage the music, how can you enjoy a party at a friend's house with a set music playlist? How will a car ride with a friend work? Music is everywhere.

A Maddux teacher once told me Daniel loved the yoga class they offered. He loved it so much he asked the teacher for a CD with the music from the class. This CD was great because sometimes Daniel would go into his room and listen to it to calm himself down if needed. So I thought it would be a great idea to bring Daniel to a local yoga studio to do a family class.

Once the class started and Daniel heard the music, he could not continue with the class because the music was not the same as at school. He told me he did not want to go back to that studio unless they used his CD.

As he has gotten older, it has become easier to explain why the limitations he places on others makes things harder on all of us. Sometimes he agrees and sometimes he does not. I think these self-imposed restrictions must be debilitating. Perhaps with more maturity he will learn to see things from other perspectives, or the desire to try new activities will be stronger than his need for rigidity. Hopefully, the hold inflexibility has on Daniel will loosen its grip and allow for him to experience more and more.

CHAPTER 10

FAMILY VACATIONS

Family vacation usually conjures images of sunshine, beaches, cocktails with umbrellas and smiling faces—emphasis on smiles on all the faces. For me, though, the thought of family vacations sometimes makes me shudder.

First, there is the packing. I write out lists and hand it to the boys. They each make piles and I look them over. As I'm squeezing all of the items into suitcases, my irrational fear overtakes me that the suitcases I specifically bought for airplane travel will not fit in the overhead compartment and we will have to check our bags and be separated from our belongings. The food and snacks I need to bring stresses me out as does knowing if the kids forget something because I forgot to put it on the list, I will be the one to blame. This has happened many times in the past. They did not pack toiletries because I did not specifically list them because I thought that was a no-brainer. The fear that the trip will not be fun, that we will have bad weather, that there will be a big fight and we will regret not being home to sulk in our own spaces can all be crippling. It's a wonder we take trips at all. But we do.

One of the places we frequent is Walt Disney World in Florida. We have made this trip multiple times for one reason:

it is Daniel's happy place. Daniel absolutely loves Disney. In fact, he specifically asked me to include a chapter about Disney in this book. Daniel loves going on the rides that create an immersive environment.

We do prep for our trips. We watch movies the rides are based on like *Haunted Mansion* starring Eddie Murphy, all the *Pirates of the Caribbean* movies, the newest of the *Star Wars* series, *The Mandalorian*, and most of the animated Disney movies. Daniel will tell you that "the Haunted Mansion was a ride first and they decided to make a movie based on the ride after the success of the *Pirates of the Caribbean* movies. But the *Haunted Mansion* movie ended up being a flop."

Daniel knows facts about all the rides in the parks and has a plan before we even get there. He knows which parks he wants to visit first and has an order for the rides. One year, we had to get to Disney because Daniel had read on the internet that a ride called Splash Mountain may be rethemed. We had to get there before the Splash Mountain ride was repurposed for a different movie. Sometimes Disney will swap out rides or get rid of them all together like they did for Lilo and Stitch. Daniel was happy to see that ride leave the park as it was not our favorite.

We keep returning to Disney World because it has an amazing inclusion program. This makes it one of the easiest places for us to go. Because we've been there multiple times, I, the planner, am less stressed because I generally know what to expect. Disney has a program called Disability Assistance Service (DAS) for people with cognitive differences that helps manage waiting in the long lines for popular rides. This program allows us to skip the physical waiting. We still have to wait the same amount of time, but we don't have to stand in the queue.

One year, just Daniel and I went to Florida because Seth had a different spring break than Daniel. Disney with Daniel is no joke. He knows which rides he wants to ride and how many times. He has certain items he brings from home so he can create a similar with his own item and something at the park. He has watched all the rides on YouTube so many times that he memorized every scene of every ride and knows the music that plays in each section.

A lot of excitement surrounds our trips. The great thing about Disney is that they are very interested in making your experience the best it can be. I have learned that at Disney, if Daniel really wants something, I should ask one of the people in the Customer Representative's office. Sometimes they say no, but more often than not, they will try to accommodate.

One day, Daniel and I were on the Haunted Mansion ride and it got stuck. This was not that big of a deal, but some rowdy kids were on another dune buggy. Even though they were not allowed to get out of their seats, they got out and were running around banging on other dune buggies, including ours. This was a bit unnerving because the ride is mostly in the dark.

When the ride started up again and we were able to get out, I asked the person working there if it was possible for us to go on it again because the banging was very unnerving and it upset my son. I asked if it was possible to ride it without having to wait in the long line or getting a return time. I made it clear that I was not trying to take advantage of the system but that Daniel had literally planned his whole Disney day around this ride, and it had been ruined by the rowdy boys. Daniel's plan could not be altered as a plan is law to a kid on the spectrum. The employee was so nice and understanding that he gave us a pass to skip the line and go through again. He told Daniel to have a great time. No judgment and no irritation.

At Hollywood Studios, Daniel loves the Star Tours ride, but I can't ride it more than once because it gives me motion sickness. The people who worked the ride, called cast members, saw that Daniel loved it and was riding it repeatedly. A cast member also noticed my face was turning greener. They allowed me to sit in the waiting area and told Daniel he could stay in his seat and go on the ride over and over without having to get back in line. I was immensely grateful and loved the understanding and special attention Daniel received. I didn't have to ask for special favors. They just wanted to help us out. That was a memory maker. Daniel still talks about that time.

Toward the end of our trip, we went to Animal Kingdom. Daniel wanted to ride the Na'avi River ride, and the Dinosaur ride. These rides are on opposite ends of the park. The way the DAS system worked then was that once you rode the ride you waited for, you'd go to the next ride to get a return time. This meant we would go to Na'avi, get a return time, go to It's Tough to be a Bug, which is in the middle of the park and usually has little or no wait, then go back to ride Na'avi.

After that, we would walk to Dinosaur, get a return time, and go back to It's Tough to be a Bug to kill time. After a while, I wised up and sent Daniel on Dinosaur alone. Then I would run back with his wrist band to Na'avi. I clocked a lot of steps running back and forth. Eleven miles. I walked eleven miles in one day.

So, I took a chance. I went to customer service and I asked if it was at all possible for Daniel to come back tomorrow morning before our flight and just ride Dinosaur multiple times.

When I make special requests, I always tell the person that if the request is too difficult for them, I will completely accept a no. I want them to know that I am not impossible to deal with. Then, I explained to them what I had been doing all week, running back and forth, following their rules and clocking many miles. I explained that we were leaving the next day, and we wouldn't have time to run back and forth and that Dinosaur was the only ride Daniel wanted to ride.

I think they saw the desperation in my face and calculated what I call the "fun to trouble ratio" and they agreed. They asked me how many times Daniel wanted to ride it and I said no fewer than three. I walked out with five passes to ride Dinosaur, and I was relieved knowing that we did Disney to the fullest and would make the flight without a problem. Finding places with accommodations and people who are willing to support us makes our vacations much easier. And I appreciate every bit of it.

Another place with an inclusion program is Hershey Park. They have a similar system for managing the wait times and are also very accommodating. On a recent trip, we went to ride the Reese's Cupfusion. This was a newer ride at the time and typically had a long line. To entertain the people waiting, they had large TV screens all around the area streaming animated two-minute video clips starring the characters from the ride. It started with an orange Reese's peanut butter cup that talks for a few minutes about the ride. Mint, the villain, took over for a few minutes, and a few other characters would speak. These video clips are on a loop, five segments total, which is a total of ten minutes.

Daniel said he wanted to record the animation clips. I saw no harm in this and knew this was one of his goals for the trip, so I let him. He stood next to a screen for ten minutes recording the sequence. Afterward, he did not look very happy. He explained the audio was not good, and he needed to get closer to a speaker. Short of climbing on a ladder and holding the video camera to the ceiling, we really had no good way to get quality sound. Daniel had already written a letter to the Hershey offices to ask for audio files of these clips but had not heard back.

Our next step was to find the best speaker, one we could physically get close to without having to hang from the ceiling. Having a child on the spectrum means he thinks nothing of going through the space looking for a speaker he can reach. His solutions don't consider the other people involved. He doesn't think about how everyone else waiting for this ride would probably be unhappy with a kid pushing his way through an already established line. To these people, it would appear as if Daniel was trying to cut the line not that he was on a mission to find the best speaker.

This is where I come in. I am the voice of reality. I explained to Daniel that it was not a very good idea to go through the line of people. I decided to enlist help. I found a ride employee and explained the scenario. I asked if the employee could escort my son as he looked for a viable speaker. I was met with a confused, "What? What do you want to do?" But I am very used to this and unaffected. I just rephrased and expounded on my request. After a bit more explaining, Daniel was paired with a staff member wearing a bright orange Cupfusion uniform and walking through the line.

Unfortunately, none of the speakers were good enough for Daniel. Desperate to get out of this situation, I tried to problem solve. The issue was if Daniel recorded the video, he couldn't get close enough to the speaker. If he sat by the speaker, he could no longer record the video. I suggested that he do this separately. I asked him if it was possible to strip the audio off a file and sync it with a video. He said yes. So now, all we had to do was record separately. But that would take twenty more minutes, and I would have to see these videos loop two more times. To save myself time and sanity, I suggested that we do one or the other.

Since I knew I was unable to find a good enough speaker, I suggested Daniel again be escorted by a uniformed staff member and record the audio while I recorded the video on my phone. This is how I found myself standing in the middle of a line, with people walking around me, my arms raised above my head to record the looping video for ten minutes. That was a long time to have my arms up in the air. An iPhone can get quite heavy after about two minutes. The man standing at the end of the line, who kind of knew what was going on, looked on encouragingly. Others passed by wondering what in the world I was doing. Daniel checked on me between the short breaks to make sure I was doing it right. When those videos ended, I was elated. We were finally able to leave the ride and move on to the next situation—again, all thanks to the incredible inclusion-minded staff who worked at Hershey Park.

Not all vacations are chosen by Daniel, and these take some cajoling to get Daniel to be on board. Since leaving him home alone is not an option, he joins us sometimes happily, sometimes grumpily. As Daniel finished his freshman year in high school, we drove to Boston for our nephew's bar mitzvah with the intention to visit Martha's Vineyard for a week afterward. Unfortunately, because our plans were very last minute, the house we were able to rent was not a pet-friendly one. I knew Daniel would want Lucky there, and I wanted the dog there because he helps when Daniel is bored. Daniel can always walk the dog, snuggle with the dog, and play with the dog. Lucky is a good distraction for Daniel so he does not seek negative attention from other members of the family. Also, we love Lucky immensely.

Knowing Daniel was going to be a bit stuck on having the dog come with us to Martha's Vineyard, I had looked into getting Lucky certified as an emotional support dog. This enables Lucky to be in restaurants, fly with us, stay with us in hotels, and accompany us wherever support animals are permitted. Lucky is not a service dog. Those dogs are specially trained to serve their owners. Lucky is there to support Daniel emotionally. Lucky is there when Daniel is anxious and there to calm Daniel down when he is upset. Lucky is the literal definition of an emotional support animal.

After I established Lucky as such and discussed the legitimacy of this status with two developmental pediatricians, I asked the real estate company if we could bring our very small Cockapoo. The company said no. I asked if it was possible to let him stay with us because he is an emotional support animal, and our son would really benefit from him being there. The company said no.

We were all disappointed, but we pressed on. We left Lucky with my in-laws and listened to Daniel's, "Why can't Lucky come with us? Mama, I really want Lucky to come with us. Remember when he came with us to the other beach rental? Mom, Lucky loves the beach. Mama…"

We got off the ferry to Martha's Vineyard, drove to the rental house, and unlocked the door per our instructions. The first thing I tripped over was a huge metal dog bowl. It was not the size for a small Cockapoo but a large bowl. We looked around and saw dog toys, dog scratches, even dog hair on some of the decorative pillows. To say the kids were confused is an understatement.

I immediately picked up the phone and called the real estate agent. I said the first thing we saw in this house were huge dog bowls. Maybe since the owners have such a large dog, they would not mind if our small, hypoallergenic, well-trained, certified emotional support animal joined us. I asked them to please call the owners and ask if we could pay an extra deposit, pay for damages if any occurred, or pay extra in rent to have our dog. The company said no.

I was beyond exasperated. But part of being a parent is modeling good behavior, so I accepted the no as a final answer. I reported to the kids there was no possibility of Lucky coming to stay with us. Both boys were very disappointed. Daniel looked at me and said, "But, Mama, did you offer them money?"

The scene from *The Princess Bride,* where Inigo says to the six-fingered man, "Offer me money! Power too, promise me that!" flashed through my head. I told Daniel I had offered them lots of money and lots of options but they still said no. Sometimes that is the end, and we must accept it.

Later, I reflected on that conversation. My son, who gets very frustrated if I ask him about life skills questions (e.g., if you have to be somewhere at x time, at what time should you start getting ready? Leave the house?), actually gets life pretty well. Asking me about offering money showed a sophistication I didn't know he had acquired. These moments always fascinate me. Perhaps he is savvier than I realize. This line of thinking about the future and how it will be for Daniel can send me on an anxiety spiral. I have to stop myself and send my thoughts in a different direction.

I also laughed to myself about how well my son knows me. Daniel knows I would never give up at the first sign of a refusal. He knows I would make several attempts to change the answer. What surprised me was he knew there was an option to offer them financial compensation. I was referring to this as an extra deposit or a pet fee, but Daniel downright called it a bribe. I laughed that we both had the same idea. But even Mom has to accept a no answer sometimes, and she will do it without a fuss. Now we flip it and turn this situation into a win or a teaching moment. Mom made multiple valiant efforts, but sometimes we can't always get what we want. This is a life lesson I often have to teach Daniel and one I'm also still working on.

Daniel can be tricky when it comes to new things. He likes things a certain way, and this becomes somewhat difficult when we travel. One doctor wisely said that Daniel is desperately trying to recreate an exact replica of the day before. At home, he likes things a certain way, but surprisingly, he has no problem sleeping in a different room, different bed, and different house when we travel. This fascinates me because I can never predict what will be an issue and what will not.

With all these minefields we navigate daily, Daniel can appear to be an ill-tempered kid. Some things set him off, yes. But if I am honest with myself, I have particular things that I dislike when I travel. I like to drink hot tea. Hotel rooms stock coffee, but they sometimes don't have tea. This bothers me a lot. Do I fixate on it? No. I just bring my own tea bags with me. Daniel happens to be more vocal about his concerns and frustrations because I am here to listen. He has a person to vent to. Not everything Daniel says is a grievance. He often says truths so genuine and from the heart they are breathtaking.

When the kids were little, Greg's dad gave Daniel a navy-blue fleece with a black dog logo on it from The Black Dog store in Martha's Vineyard. Since then, I noticed people with shirts, hats, or had car magnets with the same black dog logo. For reasons I can't really explain, I was obsessed with this Black Dog merchandise. I wanted to go to Martha's Vineyard, see the store, and buy some stuff. It was one of my goals when Greg said we should check out Martha's Vineyard.

When we got to the island, I saw the store as we drove off the ferry. I said I wanted to check out The Black Dog store during our stay. The family neither shared nor understood my need to visit this shop, but they didn't question it.

While walking around looking for grilled cheese sandwiches in Edgartown for Daniel to eat, we happened upon the sign with the black dog. Of course, I went in. I first took a selfie under the store sign. Then I took more pictures of the experience. Photos of me in the store, me shopping, the kids in the store, all of it. They all humored me and left me alone to shop. This was a dream being realized.

Leaving the store with a huge bag of t-shirts, hats, magnets, sweatshirts, and dog toys, I gleefully thanked the family for going in and shopping there and told them how it made my trip. When Mom is happy, the family is happy. Later that evening, I found out about a promotion where if you spend a certain amount at The Black Dog store, you get a free tote bag. I had not known about the promotion, so I decided to go back.

We were in the same neighborhood a few days later. I went in and saw the sign for the tote bag promotion. I told the woman behind the counter I was there a few days ago, had purchased a bunch of items, and I had not known to ask for the free tote. I asked if they would honor my receipt and give me a tote that day. I locked eyes with the woman behind the counter and she went to reach for the tote. Another attendant stood nearby, and she asked to see my receipt. I was happy to comply and I pulled out my phone. I told her I don't keep paper receipts because I lose them. So I take a picture and put them in my receipt app.

She said, "We absolutely will honor your purchase and give you a tote, but we have to check with the manager to see if an electronic receipt will suffice."

I told her I would wait. In a short time, she returned saying I was not able to get the tote. The manager wanted my hardcopy receipt and would not accept the photograph. I was speechless. They could see my credit card number printed on there and my purchases were listed. Did they think I had snapped a photo of someone else's receipt like I was trying to scam them? I was, coincidentally, wearing one of the items I had just purchased. Flustered, I left the store. I was pretty upset because I still could not understand the reason for the manager's decision. Over lunch I relayed the events to the kids and Greg. I asked their opinions as I was trying to figure it all out.

Daniel said, "Mom, do you want me to go with you to fight them?"

I laughed a little because as sweet as that was, I knew that would be a scene on the ten o'clock news. "That's really nice of you," I said. "But I think I can call them later and do some more investigating."

Daniel looked at me and said, "Mama, you look really upset. I want to go with you to fix it because you always do everything you can to make sure I have good vacations all the time."

This almost brought me to tears because he sees the truth. Even if he doesn't always act like it, he sees it, he shares it, and he knows it to be true. I love that. That comment and conversation made my trip to Martha's Vineyard one of my favorite vacations to date. I also ended up victorious in the battle of the receipts. I went back to the store and spoke to a different person. He input the data from my photo receipt into the computer and confirmed it was legitimate. He seemed truly perplexed I had had problems in the first place. With that, I walked out with my tote in hand, winning at life.

CONCLUSION

Having our diagnosis for over a decade, I feel like it's not easier or harder than when we first found out. However, I do believe we are more skilled at handling the bumps along the road. We know what to do when we encounter hiccups, and we are reassured by the wins—big and small. We know we will always have unique experiences every single day.

Daniel, in high school, is now a full head taller than me at about five feet, ten inches. Yet I'm still banging my head on the floor in frustration.

"Daniel, wow," I say. "You need to *patchin patchin* your toenails. They are super long." In Japanese, we use onomatopoeias to describe many things. *Patchin patchin* is the sound a nail clipper makes, so that is what we call cutting nails.

"No, I can't," Daniel says, "because I only *patchin patchin* when I get a haircut."

Annoyed, I ask, "Can you just *patchin patchin*? Please don't be difficult."

Daniel replies harshly, "No, I only *patchin patchin* when I get my hair cut and I can't get my hair cut until I get my wires in my braces after my spacers come out."

We had been having such a nice time discussing all the merits of the new Reese's ride versus the old one (P.S. how dare they change the ride on us). Daniel had been going on and on, talking like he was an expert. And then *bam*! I can't get him to cut his nails because he has firmly associated it with cutting his hair, which is now somehow linked to his braces.

One time, filled with exasperation and defeat, I hollered at Greg, "I'm so sorry I have gone and broken the children!" To which he shouted back, "That's okay, Kur, you only *half* broke the kids. I did the other half." It was a simple reminder that we are in it together. There's no one to blame. A couple who breaks their children together fifty-fifty is a couple who stays together. It could become a saying. Some days, when I'm in less of a humorous mood, I simply declare defeat. I quit. Mom is officially cancelled. And I curl up in a fetal position on the floor.

This is the thing about autism, or more specifically, *our* autism. I can never guess when or how it will strike. Sometimes, I have the patience. Sometimes, I curl up in my comfortable hiding spot under multiple blankets with my phone and watch one of my shows to block everything else out. I am, however, less angry. I have accepted the fact that I have a very unique and also very sweet child. He's on the spectrum and I know we will have days I do not understand anything he is saying or thinking. I have learned to stay calm and focus on the now.

I try never to ask why. Who cares why? It's just a thing. Haircuts and cutting nails and now braces—there may never be a why. Searching for an answer has led me down many a dark and winding spiral. I don't even really care why anymore. For example, Daniel cannot stand to be touched by someone with their sleeves pushed up. If you try to touch him with long sleeves pushed or rolled up, he will jerk away like he was zapped by electricity. I used to want to know why. Now, I just add it to the list of things he can't stand.

I can hear the therapists in my head saying don't accept it. Help him get over it. Try to get him used to being touched with your sleeves up. Try touching him first with your sleeve down and then slowly move it higher. I have decided some things are not worth it. These are personal decisions I make as the person who knows Daniel the best. Therapists have awesome ideas and great tips. I love to hear ideas from both professionals and other parents. But in the end, some things I let go because it is not worth it. It's okay to say, "So what?" It's okay to curl up in a ball on the floor and not force my son to cut his nails. There will be other days when I may press the issue, but I think as the person living the life, Daniel and I get to make the final call on what to work on.

Conversations with fellow parents of children on the spectrum can be a fountain of information—a place to get ideas and hear other people's creative solutions. I am always curious to hear about the unique quirks other children have, or had, and also the steps they've taken to change the behavior. I've heard of kids opening and closing sliding doors, lining up anything that can be put in a row, opening all manner of bottles within reach, running back and forth along one side of a room, and much more. I like to learn what others have tried, what has had success, and what has failed. I confess, I sometimes prefer to hear about the failures more than the successes. It makes me feel reassured that other people are as lost as I am and still trying like we are.

I am the first to admit I am not perfect. I also know that I am, at times, the instigator. Many tantrums could have been avoided if I had not been immature or impatient or unwilling to be the adult. I sometimes find myself fighting with Daniel as if I were a sullen, stubborn, and mean teenager. I wish I was able to say I am blessed with a child on the spectrum, and it has made me a better person. I wish I could say I love autism for teaching me to see things differently.

The poem "Welcome to Holland" by Emily Perl Kingsley talks about having a child with a disability. She says it's like planning a trip to Italy and having all of those expectations and dreams but ending up in Holland. Holland is a different experience. It's still great—just not what you expected. I am not like that. I'm the one kicking and screaming at the airport demanding to be put on the plane to Italy. It's hard for me to accept my Holland, and I am not very proud of that.

The worry often has me paralyzed. I worry all the time about the safety of my children. I wonder if the inability to read a room or a situation will put Daniel in actual danger. I want to be worry free in Italy, but I'm stuck in Holland with a suitcase filled with anxiety. The constant worry, the fear of the unknown, and what *could* happen is debilitating. Worrying about our children is part of being a parent even though history has shown me I don't need to be so terrified. Worried? Yes. But code-red terrified? Probably not. We'll eventually have to let go so he can figure it out. I'm just not sure I can do that.

I worry constantly about my son making friends, knowing what to say, and knowing how to be. I wonder if the friendships he has are reciprocated. Every time Daniel has been thrown into a new situation, and I grew an ulcer worrying about the outcome, he has risen to the occasion. Every. Single. Time. We always have bumps in the road, and sometimes he gets some help from me or others, but Daniel has not tried to do one single thing that he has not conquered.

In the beginning, these were little things. Will he be able to drink water from a straw? Yes, he did. Will he be able to learn how to read? Yes, he did. Will he be able to make it at Homerun Baseball camp for the day without a shadow? Yes, he did. Would he successfully conquer riding a bike without training wheels? Yes, he did. Would he be able to make it at a new school in third grade? Yes, he did. Could he learn to read the Torah and celebrate his bar mitzvah? With enormous success. Could he earn his black belt in martial arts? Yes, and we have the first-degree black belt and certificate hanging on his wall. Could he make it at a public high school (with a class size of approximately six hundred students per grade) after only being in tiny private schools all of his life? Yes, he sure did, and he likes it more than the smaller schools. Could he make it three weeks at sleepaway camp without the comforts of home, his favorite foods, his phone, and without contacting his mom? Yes, he did and wants to go back.

I am immensely proud of Daniel for what he continues to overcome. I hope for more and more successes in the future for him and for any child on the spectrum. For any child. Period.

Has being the mom of a child on the spectrum made me a better person? Maybe. Or maybe I would have become a better person regardless. How would I ever know? I know I am the person who will go to a party and seek out the man or woman who looks awkward, socially uncomfortable, and alone to go chat with. I do this not because I am a nice person, but I know my son will be in this situation one day. Maybe if I pay it forward here, someone might do the same for Daniel when he needs it. Maybe once everyone is comfortable with the idea of autism, I won't have to worry so much. But until then, I will always look out for the loner in the pack.

Being the parent of a child on the spectrum is not easy. We still have no cure and no way of understanding the how or why. I have an impossibly hard time explaining things in a way that gets through to my son consistently. Some days are definitely worse than others, but the feelings of fear and hopelessness dissipate somewhat if I remember to recount and celebrate the successes of how we got where we are today.

I think we need to work on plenty of things—more classes to attend and more learning to be done. But we all need to work on ourselves all the time. Anything that will make my son's life easier is something to take on as a challenge. Being able to try or even tolerate more varieties of food is a major one. This would enable Daniel to broaden his scope of activities, travel, go out to meals with friends, and open up more opportunities to socialize. But Daniel is an incredible human. I don't think he should change anything about himself that makes him uniquely Daniel.

Feeling like an outsider is tough for anyone at any age. Walking into a party not knowing anyone is a hard thing to do. And once you get to that party, and you sit in a chair to join a group of friends, you're still not really part of the group yet. Physically you are sitting in the group, but there's one more step. You join that circle once you laugh together at a joke, share one of your own, tell a story or two, ask or answer a few questions, and spend some time getting to know each other. That's when you can feel like part of the circle.

Most people think inviting someone to join them is "inclusion" because you are, in fact, including them. For many, just having a seat at the table is enough to be brought into the fold. This is not the same for people who have social skills deficits. They need a hook to pull them into the conversation. I think this key difference makes inclusion so subtle and tricky. I would love it if the social norm was to invite and offer a lifeline by encouraging and helping others join the conversation.

Whenever someone new joins a circle I am in, I try to say, "Hello, we were just talking about…" as an open invitation to chime in, not just physically but with words and thoughts. Whether they choose to participate is something I have no control over. If it were my son, I wish for him with my entire heart that he would take that opportunity to jump in, say some words, and share his thoughts. I want nothing more than for my boys to be included in a community and into life so they can experience it fully and feel accepted.

This autism journey is unique to us, and we work through it by plowing forward every day. This is our life and our experiences. This journey is about us, Daniel and me. My son may never eat a plate of sushi with me, but that's fine because we can spend hours in front of the piano playing name that tune. We will always find ways to stay connected. We may even start operation white rice one day in the future.

ACKNOWLEDGMENTS

Thank you to Daniel for letting me tell our story. I know it took a lot of courage to let me write this book. Thank you to Seth for letting me bounce ideas off of you and encouraging me to continue. I love our conversations and hearing your insights. Thank you to Greg for your support and for always being in my corner. You keep Team Levine grounded. There is no one I'd rather do life with than you.

Ericka, thank you for our daily chats and helping me laugh at it all.

Anne, thank you for being the easiest family to travel with and accepting all that comes with us.

Annalisa, thank you for being the best cheerleader and for telling me to get the dog.

Carolyn, thank you for always making me food and letting me vent on our walks.

Crystal, thank you for sharing so many meals with me and a love of pies and sweets.

Traci, thank you for writing your book which inspired me to want to write mine.

Thank you to Team Daniel and all of the teachers, counselors, therapists, and doctors who helped get us here. Each of you has taught me something special along the way. Thank you for helping mold Daniel into the fine human he is becoming.

Thank you to my in-laws who came with Greg. Thank you for bringing me into the fold as part of the family. Abby, thank you for telling me what was what in the beginning. I truly am grateful.

To Mom and Dad, thank you for teaching me how to be me.

To my brother, Atchan. Dude, I'd rob a bank for you, too. Well, I'd rather not, but I can't have you one-up me. You're the best brother and I hope my boys have the same kind of relationship we do.

Thank you to my editors and publishers.

Leilani Squires, thank you for your patience and input.

Eric Koester, thank you for the boot camp and seeing potential in my twenty thousand words.

Kathy Wood, thank you for keeping your cool when I was cancelled. Your advice and organization got this project completed.

Thank you to New Degree Press for turning my thoughts into an actual book.

APPENDIX

CHAPTER 2
Seuss, Dr. *Dr. Seuss's ABC*. New York: Beginner Books, 1963.

CHAPTER 5
Levinson, Barry, dir. *Rain Man*. 1988; Santa Monica, CA: United Artists.

CHAPTER 7
Vidor, King, et al. dir. *The Wizard of Oz*. 1939; United States: Metro-Goldwyn-Mayer (MGM).

CHAPTER 9
Hoopmann, Kathy. *All Cats Have Asperger Syndrome*. London: Kingsley, Jessica Publishers, 2006.

CHAPTER 10
Minkoff, Rob, dir. *The Haunted Mansion*. 2003; United States: Walt Disney Home Entertainment.
Reiner, Rob, dir. *The Princess Bride*. 1987; United States: Twentieth Century Fox.

www.ingramcontent.com/pod-product-compliance
Lightning Source LLC
LaVergne TN
LVHW010331070526
838199LV00065B/5722